SOCIAL ISSUES AND THE
LOCAL CHURCH

Social Issues and the
Local Church

Edited by

Ian Shaw

EVANGELICAL PRESS OF WALES

© Evangelical Press of Wales, 1988
First published 1988
ISBN 1 85049 046 5

Cover photograph: The City Centre, Liverpool
By courtesy of the Britain On View Photographic Library (BTA/ETB)

The choice of version for Bible quotations was left to the individual contributors. Unless otherwise indicated, Paul Bassett has followed the Authorized Version, Gerallt Wyn Davies the Amplified Bible and Fred Hughes the Revised Standard Version; Professor MacLeod has supplied his own translation, and the remaining contributors have used the New International Version

Published by the Evangelical Press of Wales
Bryntirion, Bridgend, Mid Glamorgan, CF31 4DX
Printed by The Bath Press, Bath

Contents

About the Contributors   6

Introduction   7

Part I   Social Issues, the Bible and the Local Church

1. Christians and Neighbours   11
   Ian Shaw

2. Social Issues and the Bible   23
   Ian Shaw

3. Social Issues and the Local Church   39
   Oliver R. Barclay

Part II   The Church in the World

4. The Christian and the State   59
   Donald MacLeod

5. The Inner City   77
   Paul Bassett

6. Work and Unemployment   91
   G. Wyn Davies

7. Christian Concern for Education   105
   Fred Hughes

8. The Role of Women in the Local Church   119
   Elizabeth Catherwood

9. Social Welfare and the Local Church   135
   Peter Milsom and *Ian Shaw*

10. The Church and its Mission in the Contemporary World   151
    David Smith

Bibliography   167

Index of Scripture References   172

General Index   175

About the Contributors

Oliver R. Barclay was formerly General Secretary of the Universities and Colleges Christian Fellowship. He is the author of several books on current issues, and is still involved with the UCCF in developing professional groups.

Paul Bassett is the minister of Melbourne Hall Evangelical Church — an inner city church in Leicester.

Elizabeth Catherwood is the elder daughter of the late Dr Martyn Lloyd-Jones, and has been responsible for editing many of his books. She was a schoolteacher, and is at present the editor of the women's imprint, Prisca Books.

Gerallt Wyn Davies is Dean of the Faculty of Management and Professional Studies at Gwent College of Higher Education.

Fred Hughes formerly worked with the Association of Christian Teachers. He is presently Senior Lecturer in Religious Studies at the College of St Paul and St Mary in Cheltenham.

Donald MacLeod is Professor of Systematic Theology at the Free Church of Scotland College in Edinburgh, and editor of his denomination's magazine, *The Monthly Record.*

Peter Milsom is the minister of Deeside Evangelical Church in North Wales, where he has been involved in a number of initiatives to demonstrate social concern within the local church.

Ian Shaw is Lecturer in Social Work at University College, Cardiff.

David Smith, after a pastoral ministry in Cambridge and a period of time working with the Qua Ibo Mission in Nigeria, is presently studying in the University of Aberdeen.

Introduction

The writers of this book seek to understand and apply the Word of God to some of the most pressing problems and opportunities facing Christians in society today.

A Christian approach to issues of politics, the state, education, work, the inner city, women in the church, social welfare, missions and so on must be *radical*—it must go to the root of things. This is far from saying that we should be ruled merely by the fashion of the moment. That route—popular as it is with liberal Christianity —is not radical at all, because it has no roots to find. A radical approach must be a biblical approach. We must be eager to discover the biblical principles and apply them to issues facing us today. 'Conservative evangelical' well describes the attitude of the contributors to the authority of the Bible, but we must not carry over that conservatism in an unthinking way to every other area of life. Because the gospel has something to say about the whole of life it compels us to question much that, as non-Christians, we took for granted.

A biblically radical approach will also be a *practical* one. For most Christians the problems of schooling, unemployment, single parents, poverty and so on face us not on the wider social stage but in our families, neighbourhoods, places of work and churches. Many books on social issues are written for the specialist— teachers, doctors, academics, social workers, etc. While there is an important place for specialist writing, we are concerned to offer something which most interested Christians can read and find helpful. Thus, the writers of this book ask what *we* should be doing, in *our* churches, *now*. However, the book is not written for the reader who wants a predigested set of prescriptions that can be waved like a spiritual wand over our problems. The suggestions for further reading and questions for discussion at the end of every chapter are intended to enhance the usefulness of the book as a basis for Bible studies and discussion groups in churches, house meetings and Christian Unions.

Viewing the Christian's social accountability from the standpoint of the local church provides a neglected but crucial biblical perspective. Its neglect only serves to perpetuate and widen the frequently lamented gap between the life and witness of the local church on the one hand, and demonstrations of social concern and action on the other.

Being in the world but not of the world is, for the Christian, a statement both of irreversible fact and of daily aspiration (John 17:11,14). To give well-grounded evidence of the fact, and to provoke and realize the aspiration, are the twin aims of this book.

IAN SHAW

PART I

Social Issues, the Bible and the Local Church

1

Christians and Neighbours

IAN SHAW

'IF anyone is in Christ, he is a new creation; the old has gone, the new has come!' (2 Cor. 5:17). No more radical statement of the Christian's new life can be found anywhere in the New Testament. The Christian's life has a unity and coherence—a new basic disposition behind all outward actions.

The Christian is the salt of the earth. Jesus' words immediately imply a description of the world in which we find ourselves. It is a world tending always to decay and pollution. Left to itself it goes downwards and not upwards (Rom. 1:18-32). But this world is not to be left to itself. Every Christian is to act as salt, hindering the decay and pollution, and seeking to bring individuals and structures under the preserving influence of God's truth. This will not happen unless the Christian is radically different from the world. We cannot influence the world by adopting its standards. We will only be a salting influence in so far as we are poor in spirit, meek, hungering and thirsting after righteousness, and peace-makers (Matt. 5).

The responsibility is sobering, the privilege awesome. It is only as we exhibit this Christlikeness that we will be salt in the society around us, manifesting what has been called a Christian counter-culture. Our faith must not remain a private affair. 'Christian salt has no business to remain snugly in elegant little ecclesiastical salt-cellars; our place is to be rubbed into the secular community . . . to stop it going bad' (J. Stott).[1]

NEIGHBOUR-RELATIONS

Man was created in relation to God, to himself, to his neighbour, to the created order and to time itself. When Adam and Eve sinned, their sin affected all of these relationships. From that point on, people were unfit for God's presence, filled with an inner shame and restlessness, at odds with their fellows, out of harmony with the natural order, and confronted with the reality of death. For the Christian, however, the redemption purchased by Christ affects all of these marred relationships.

God made a helper suitable for Adam because it was not good for him to be alone. The question 'Am I my brother's keeper?' (Gen. 4:9) would never have been asked before the Fall, but a broken relationship with God immediately affects our relationship with our fellow human beings. This simultaneous alienation from God and those around is underlined by Adam's bitter complaint, 'The woman you put here with me—she gave me some fruit from the tree, and I ate it' (Gen. 3:12). The murder of Abel only brought that alienation to its appalling fruition (Gen. 4:1-16). Misunderstanding, racial prejudice, social divisions, shattered families, poor labour relations and divided churches are all part of this bitter fruit of separation from our neighbour.

Redemption provides the healing for this separation. Not only are we reconciled to God, but 'in Christ we who are many form one body, and each member belongs to all the others' (Rom. 12:5). For example, Zechariah anticipates the pouring out of the Holy Spirit, and the spirit of repentance that will herald the gospel. The gospel will be universal and all-pervasive. It will reach the house of David, the chief civil power, and the house of Nathan, an insignificant, unimportant relative of the king; it will grip the house of Levi, the chief religious family, and the house of Shimei, an unimportant grandson of Levi (Zech. 12:12-14). In other words, the gospel is to permeate every social stratum, unhindered by tribal or class barriers. One test of the extent to which the Holy Spirit is at work today is the degree to which social barriers of this kind are overcome in the church.

Of course, the fact that we are Christians does not mean that we will be right in all we think and do. Our reach exceeds our grasp, and our qualified successes often seem like failure. 'What I want to do I do not do, but what I hate I do' (Rom. 7:15). Indeed, one of the remarkable things about becoming a Christian is that it almost always raises new problems which the believer has hitherto never had to confront. Just because the gospel has something to say about the whole of life, it compels us to question much that in our unbelief we had taken for granted. That is one good reason why evangelical Christians should never be found unthinkingly defending conservative positions on the role of the state, education, women in the church, labour relations, social action, the inner city, law and order, and so on, *simply because they are conservative positions*. As with one of the major campaigning organizations for prisoners of conscience, we should be against injustice (and, we would add, submissively seeking to apply the Word of God) left, right and centre.

IMAGE OF GOD

But herein lies a danger. A biblical ethic in all these areas must never be defined in terms of what believers, or, still worse, the professing church, happens to believe or do. Because the best of Christians are sinners still, our attention must be focused on divine demand, not human achievement—a divine demand that comes to men and women made in the image of God. 'The most mysterious yet glorious truth about human nature is this: that each individual, male or female, old or young, sophisticated or rough, handsome or ugly, brilliant or slow of mind, outstanding or ordinary, bears God's image' (J. I. Packer).[2] The implications are clear and far-reaching. Man has dignity and worth and merits our utmost respect. As Stuart Olyott has aptly remarked, 'You see more of the beauty of God in a bus queue than in the whole of Snowdonia.' Again, the image of God points to each man's true destiny, fulfilled only in obedience to God. While we must give full weight to God's sovereignty and acknowledge also the influences of nature and upbringing, man in the image of God still has freedom of choice and the accountability which goes with it. As Christians, therefore, we need always to cultivate informed and sensitive consciences which have been educated by the Bible.

However, a cursory reading of much contemporary Christian literature on social issues soon reveals that the idea of the image of God has been used to form the basis for many theological positions. It is on the basis of this doctrine that evangelical Christians have argued both for and against capital punishment, the ordination of women, state welfare, and capitalism. Indeed, it seems increasingly plain that in the search for common ground with the unbeliever, this aspect of biblical teaching is being asked to bear a superstructure of social ethics far more extensive than a plain reading of God's Word would warrant. The error springs in part from giving too much weight to general principles of Scripture, and not enough weight to the ways in which Scripture itself applies them. That leads us directly to the nature of the authority of God's Word in this whole area. We shall examine this in more detail in the following chapter.

The doctrine of the image of God does, of course, have a bearing on contemporary issues like relationships between the sexes, race relationships, soccer violence and many aspects of politics and ecology. For example, soccer hooligans at Brussels and elsewhere

13

are not, as many claim, animals who should be treated as such, but free and accountable individuals who should be treated accordingly. The same doctrine helps to explain why the Christian may occasionally end up fighting the same corner with the atheist, even though his motives are fundamentally different. Precisely because the law of God is written on his heart, the unbeliever has points of contact with the Christian (Rom. 2:14-15). As David Field has helpfully put it, 'The atheist . . . derives his knowledge of human rights and values from the God he says he does not believe in . . . He shares my knowledge of God-derived human responsibilities and values simply because he is created in the image of the God he rejects.'[3]

JUSTICE AND RIGHTEOUSNESS

With a conscience thus moulded by the Word of God, the Christian's witness ought to be characterized by justice and righteousness. We are not to be like the Jews of Amos's day (Amos 5:21-24) who were 'praying on their knees in the temple, and preying on their neighbours everywhere else' (J. A. Motyer).[4] They had their religious feasts with their accompanying array of sacrifices and singing, but God turned His back and would not listen. There was no right behaviour in their relationships with others—no justice which is the outward fruit of that inward righteousness before God. Hence, they were all too ready, as Derek Kidner has remarked, 'to combine sacred rites with social wrongs.'[5] Yet as Christians we ought to take encouragement from the fact that, while justice and righteousness are God's unyielding demands ('let justice roll on like a river, righteousness like a never-failing stream'—Amos 5:24), they are also God's covenant gifts to His people. 'I will betroth you to me for ever; I will betroth you in righteousness and justice, in love and compassion' (Hos. 2:19).

Amos and Hosea are not suggesting—as may almost be the case with some evangelicals today—that we should discard religion and take up morality and ethics. Social ethics are but the outflow of religion, and not its foundation. It is showing our faith by what we do (James 2:18), so that the Christian, as someone has said, is the person who does the spiritual thing naturally and the natural thing spiritually. 1 Peter 4:10-11 is helpful here. Grateful regard to *God* for gifts given, whether of ministry of the Word or of serving (v.11), must show itself in service to *others* (v.10). In this context, service to one's neighbour *is* service to God. Righteousness is the foundation of justice, just as, conversely, godlessness is the precursor of wickedness (Rom. 1:18). The same point can be made in a different way by reminding ourselves that, while love to our neighbour fulfils the law and is directed by it (Rom. 13:8-10; 1 John 5:2), love of God has priority over neighbour love and is not wholly a matter of loving our neighbour (Matt. 22:37-40).

The general principles are therefore quite clear. In practice, however, matters do not always seem so straightforward. What is right and just in this particular situation? How do I know whether my conscience is sensitive to God's Word? How should I apply general principles to the opportunity or problem facing me? Later chapters address these questions in relation to specific areas of the Christian life. For the moment I want to show that part of the answer lies in following the guidance of the Word of God about how we should resolve moral dilemmas.

MORAL DILEMMAS

In the Christian life we are sometimes faced with acute dilemmas, where the moral absolutes of the Word of God appear to be in conflict with each other. A Christian may be convinced that he or she is called to the mission field, but he is an only child and keenly aware of his responsibilities to elderly parents. Once on the mission field, parents may be faced with a choice between separation from their children in a far-away school or watching their education suffer because of their parents' call to work in a developing country. Very differently, how are we to counsel a newly converted man or woman, who wrongly deserted the partner and children of a first marriage, has now remarried and has children by the second marriage? Other examples could easily be multiplied—abortion where the mother's life is at risk, ministerial secession from denominational affiliation, and so on. A familiar historical example is Captain Oates's decision to take his own life by walking out of the tent sheltering Scott's returning Antarctic party, in the hope that he would thus enable the others to reach safety.

Biblical examples of moral dilemmas also exist. Both Daniel and his three friends had to resolve conflicts between obedience to the state and faithfulness to God (Dan. 3; 6). Abraham turned Hagar and Ishmael out of his home, and proved himself ready to kill his own son. The fact that God directed him in both cases did not remove the pain of the dilemmas (Gen. 21:8-14; 22). On their return from Babylon, the Israelites were faced with divorcing their foreign wives and were 'greatly distressed by the occasion' (Ezra 10:9).

15

How are we to determine the way we should act in such circumstances? Perhaps the most important point to make is that in the majority of cases we are not faced with a true dilemma. Usually, the conflict is a straightforward one between God's will and our sinful reluctance to follow Him. In other words, what we need in such cases is not clearer divine guidance but simple obedience. We must beware of inventing non-existent moral dilemmas.

Many Christians would go further and argue that in every case we only face apparent dilemmas. Thus, in answer to the question, 'Is it ever right to lie to save a life?' (e.g. Josh. 2:4,5; Exod. 1:15-22), the answer would be that lying is always wrong, and there will always be a way of obeying all of God's commands. In the case of Rahab and the spies, truth-telling may have been compatible with protecting the spies; but in the case of the Hebrew midwives, who disobeyed the state and lied to cover their disobedience, we are told that God was kind to them because they feared Him. We seem to be faced with a situation here (and in the case of Daniel and his friends) where disobedience to the state was the right course of action.[6] In other words, the Christian is sometimes faced with circumstances where he has to choose the greater good. The resolution of conflicting demands between the mission field and family responsibilities falls into this category, as do secession from denominational affiliations and abortion where the mother's life is at risk. Captain Oates's action was of a similar kind, although made the more painful because he could not be certain that it would achieve any benefit.

Christ dealt with a similar issue when the disciples were criticized by the Pharisees for picking and eating corn on the sabbath. He referred to Old Testament examples of similar behaviour by God's people who 'yet are innocent' (Matt. 12:1-8). In such situations we are not to think that by seeing the right answer we are freed from the pain of the situation. Although we may *regret* having to do certain things, we need not *repent*. We may not think that we have done a *good* thing, but we will have the confidence that it is just and righteous.

However, some dilemmas are caused by our sin, and the solution is not free of sin. The example of a newly converted man or woman with a history of broken marriage falls into this category. The biblical examples of divorcing foreign wives and turning out Hagar and Ishmael may also be cited (Ezra 9; 10; Gen. 21). In such cases no course is entirely free of sin, and we are to do the lesser evil with a heavy heart and seek God's cleansing of our consciences for having done it.[7]

PRINCIPALITIES AND POWERS

Christian diffidence about social involvement will be harder to sustain if we come to grips with the biblical teaching outlined so far. We can also be helped by the use of good literature, and further reading is recommended at the end of this and other chapters. Unfortunately, not all Christian writing is equally helpful. For example, some evangelicals have increasingly developed an unduly negative view of the state, due in part to what David Lyon calls 'the diverting impact of Marxism'.[8]

The idea of 'structural sin' has taken strong root among some writers, and this is often expressed in the interpretation of the words 'principalities and powers' (NIV, 'rulers and authorities') in Ephesians 3:10 and 6:12. The argument has been put forward that this refers to the structures and institutions of the state, which, like the tower of Babel, unify men in their separation from God. This is not the place to discuss such views in detail,[9] except to note the dangers in identifying the principalities and powers of Scripture with the state. John Stott makes three helpful observations. *First*, the interpretation fails to explain why some but not all structures become tyrannical. *Second*, and more important, it unjustifiably limits the activity of Satan. Indeed, one suspects that its origins lie in liberal attempts to demythologize the Bible by removing personal, demonic activity into the background. *Finally*, it reinforces the unduly negative attitude towards society and its structures that we noted above, so that the state becomes regarded as almost automatically in the wrong. 'Advocates of the new theory warn us against deifying structures; I want to warn them against demonising them.'[10] We need to realize that the state as such is neither divine nor demonic, but is God's servant. This remains true whether rulers recognize the fact or not. It is also true despite those evil aspects of the state against which we must guard.

THE LOCAL CHURCH

One of the main aims of this book is to draw attention to the outworking of social concern within the local church. What follows is a ground-clearing exercise to discover why the relationship of social issues to the local church has been so little emphasized or appreciated.

Scripture and Church Government

Social issues have often been debated in the most lively fashion by evangelicals who do not hold in any strong way to what has been called the regulative principle—the belief that Scripture has authority over church government as well as over doctrine and practice. Hence, they are likely to regard the application of biblical teaching as very much a matter for each church. Joyce Baldwin gives expression to this view in her discussion of women's ministry when she writes, 'In matters of organisation and structure local churches are free to adopt whatever pattern is appropriate for their circumstances.'[11]

The contributors to this book would doubtless hold different positions over the doctrine of the 'gathered church', but they would be united in believing that the New Testament does have something to say about organization and structure that is regulative for local church life.

Suspicions of the Church

It is rather difficult to substantiate, but I believe that some evangelicals concerned about social issues have a mistrust of the local church. They may even have withdrawn from active participation in a local evangelical church or replaced it with a new community.[12]

It is both a cause and a result of trends such as these that much thinking and practice has taken place in para-church organizations and communities, or through specialist bodies. This has paradoxically served to reinforce the very divorce between social initiatives and salvation that these Christians are so quick to repudiate! We must not simply dismiss this reaction, or even assume that there is no place for the exercise of special gifts. While all Christians are to act as salt and light, not every person is gifted for active involvement in social affairs, but *some* should be as a matter of God's gift and calling (see Oliver Barclay's chapter on this theme). Neither are we to conclude that social action should only take place through the local church. Much will be done through individuals and also through collaboration between churches. But a crucial dimension of this social involvement must be the local church.

Revival and Social Concern

In response to a recent survey of unemployment in Welsh churches, one pastor replied that a God-given revival is the only answer to our problems. Unemployment, he believed, is in the last analysis a product of the nation's departure from God and His laws. How are we to respond to this? Even if unemployment, or whatever else may be our concern, is not *solely* a product of spiritual apostasy, can we not say amen to the vision of this pastor and many like him?

18

The tension is a real one. If we do not feel any tension between social concern and prayer for revival—or more broadly between prayer and social concern—there is something defective in our spiritual vision. For we do need revival, and that awareness is all too absent in much talk about social involvement. The kind of concern expressed by the pastor quoted above seems to spring largely from a fear that, at root, social involvement is a species of legalism, of salvation by works; and indeed, in so far as prayer is missing, legalism has a head start.

However, to abandon social concern and wait for revival is to run the risk of turning Christianity into mysticism. It is always wrong in any sphere of the Christian life to set prayer against action. We can see this clearly in evangelism. In the life of the church the prayer for revival and the work of reformation ought to go together. We have seen this already in thinking about justice and righteousness, where we recognized that these are God's demands to be assiduously obeyed and, at the same time, God's covenant, gracious gifts.[13] Christians who pray most for revival should also be those who are most committed to the practical implications of being salt in society.

We must move a step further. Is it a correct inference that revival, when it comes, will solve our problems? There are strong and weak versions of this argument. The stronger version claims that revival will in and of itself solve our social problems without any organized initiative by Christians. The weaker version argues that revival will lead to effective social initiatives through the Holy Spirit's sanctifying work in the lives of Christians.

There is obviously some truth in both versions of this argument, but they are far from the whole truth for three reasons. First, revival has not solved *all* social problems in the past, and we have no theological grounds for believing that revival exhausts God's purposes for social reform. That would be almost like arguing that the effects of the Fall on man's relationship to his neighbour can be entirely eradicated in the gospel age. Secondly, there has often been a marked time-lag between revival and the outworking of its social consequences. Finally, it is quite conceivable that, far from *solving* social problems, revival may even *create* social unease and 'turn the world upside down'. It may, for example, stimulate a new demand for education which neither Christians nor non-Christians have hitherto felt.

Christians are sometimes guilty of an unbiblical nostalgia (Eccles. 7:10). 'We remember [at least we *think* we remember] the fish we ate in Egypt at no cost . . .' (Num. 11:5). We believe that if revival came our problems would be solved.[14] But times of revival

19

portrayed in Scripture are a reminder that spiritual life brings problems and challenges as well as great blessings (Neh. 8—10; Acts; 1 Corinthians). To have the problems of spiritual life, however, is far better than the peace of spiritual inertia.

Persevering prayer for revival should go hand in hand with an equally persistent concern for the harmony of men and women with their neighbours. The one strengthens the other.

NOTES

1 J. Stott, *The Message of the Sermon on the Mount* (Inter-Varsity Press, 1978), p.65.
2 J.I. Packer, 'Conscience, Choice and Character', in *Law, Morality and the Bible,* ed. by B.N. Kaye and G.J. Wenham (Inter-Varsity Press, 1978), p.170.
3 D. Field, 'Rights and Responsibilities: Are They in Conflict?', *Christian Arena,* 37.4 (December 1984), p.11.
4 J.A. Motyer, *The Message of Amos* (Inter-Varsity Press, 1974), p.132.
5 D. Kidner, *The Message of Hosea* (Inter-Varsity Press, 1981), p.36.
6 See Donald MacLeod's chapter for a full discussion of the Christian's relationship to the state.
7 Does the Bible give guidance for arguing that certain values are more important or certain actions more serious than others? While a number of passages do support that general position (e.g. Matt. 5:22; 12:32; 23:23; John 19:11; Rom. 2:6; 1 Cor. 13:13), we would run the risk of legalism if we attempted to go beyond general principles. What matters is the motive of the heart — the glory of God.
8 D. Lyon, *The Steeple's Shadow* (SPCK, 1985), p.76.
9 John Stott has sounded a careful warning about this line of argument in several places, and has pointed out its exegetical and theological weaknesses, without denying that demonic intelligences can use structures and institutions for evil purposes. See, for example, Stott, *The Message of Ephesians* (Inter-Varsity Press, 1979), pp.267-75. Martyn Lloyd-Jones also pointed out that the state can become demonic — see *The Doctor Himself* (Christian Medical Fellowship, 1982), pp.60f.
10 J. Stott, *The Message of Ephesians*, p.274.
11 J. Baldwin, 'Women's Ministry — A New Look at the Biblical Texts', in *The Role of Women,* ed. by S. Lees (Inter-Varsity Press, 1984), p.175.
12 See J. Benington, *Culture, Class and Christian Beliefs* (Scripture Union, 1973), and J. Wallis, *The New Radical* (Lion Publishing, 1983).
13 See the chapter on social welfare and the local church for discussion of the related question of evangelism and a social concern.
14 'It is one thing to recognise, from a Christian perspective, the spiritual bankruptcy of much modern culture, and the often pathetic collusion of organised Christianity, in allowing itself to be shaped by such an outlook. It is another thing to assume that "once upon a time" the situation was vastly different' (Lyon, *The Steeple's Shadow*, p.18). In a fascinating book, not written from a Christian perspective, Geoffrey Pearson documents the way a widespread belief that morally things are not what they used to be has been strongly held for at least two hundred years (*Hooligan*, Macmillan, 1983).

QUESTIONS FOR DISCUSSION

a) What biblical doctrines provide a basis for social concern? What are the major tensions among evangelicals in their approach to these issues? Where do you stand?

b) Consider some of the moral dilemmas referred to in this chapter. Do the guidelines suggested here, and also in the chapter on social welfare and the local church, help you to resolve similar problems today?

c) Explore ways in which a firm belief in the centrality of the local church will shape our endeavours to be salt in society.

FURTHER READING

The most comprehensive text on social issues is John Stott's *Issues Facing Christians Today* (Marshalls, 1984). It is to be recommended, although there is no sustained application to local church life. A. N. Triton, *Salt to the World* (Inter-Varsity Press, 1978) is a very helpful exposition of general principles, drawing largely on a creation ethics approach. A more wide-ranging collection of contributions dealing with general principles can be found in *Law, Morality and the Bible* edited by B. N. Kaye and G. J. Wenham (Inter-Varsity Press, 1978). The chapters by J. I. Packer and Oliver Barclay are particularly useful. Moral dilemmas are helpfully discussed by Norman Geisler in *Options in Contemporary Christian Ethics* (Baker, 1981), although I do not go along with his rejection of the lesser evil principle.

The best books force us back to the Bible text, and commentaries are invaluable here. 'The Bible Speaks Today' series published by the Inter-Varsity Press is particularly useful. Alec Motyer's *The Message of Amos* (1974) and John Stott's volume on Ephesians (1979) have both been referred to in the chapter. Motyer's recent volume on James (1985) should also be consulted. The reader can follow up further particular points in the references cited in the text and chapter notes.

2

Social Issues and the Bible

IAN SHAW

SCRIPTURE has something relevant to say on the subject of social issues. Furthermore, as evangelical Christians we are bound by the authority of Scripture. We accept the finality, sufficiency, lucidity and harmony of the Word of God.

God's revelation is complete and sufficient. It is not a dead word but the living speech of the Holy Spirit. Scripture is the only revelation of the mind and will of God available to us. In the words of the Westminster Confession, God has revealed 'all things necessary for his own glory, man's salvation, faith and life'. To the ordinary Christian whose mind is enlightened by the Holy Spirit, the meaning of Scripture is plain. This gives the Word of God a 'commanding relevance'. Therefore, although we are to prize our spiritual heritage, 'let us know that it is not the tradition of the past, not a precious heritage, and not the labours of the fathers, that are to save this generation and this hour, but the Word of the living and abiding God deposited for us in Holy Scripture' (J. Murray).[1]

Questions may already be pressing on your mind. Does this mean that all Scripture is equally authoritative in its teaching on social issues? For example, how are we to relate the Old and New Testaments? How can we distinguish the permanent and the passing in the Word of God? Does culture matter? If so, how do we distinguish the cultural garments from the body of revelation? Put differently, does Scripture give us general principles which we in turn have to apply? If so, what guidance does Scripture itself give on how to apply the ancient Word in the modern world? At what point do differences over the *interpretation* of Scripture become differences over the *authority* of Scripture?

These and other similar questions occur to all careful readers of the Bible, but they are particularly pressing when we consider the teaching of Scripture on social issues. The effect of accepting unreservedly the authority of Scripture should be to make us work hard at such questions, and submit our minds and lives to its teaching. The sea of Scripture, as has often been observed, is shallow enough for children to paddle in, and deep enough for adults to swim in. This should steer us away from glib answers to the questions in the previous paragraph. I have a poster outside my room in college which reads,

For Every Complex Problem there is a Simple Solution — *and it's wrong*

A full discussion of the form and character of biblical teaching on social issues is beyond the scope of a single chapter. Guidance for the more ambitious reader is given at the end of the chapter. Here, we will restrict ourselves to a preliminary consideration of four closely linked issues. These are: applying the principles of God's Word, the relation of the two Testaments, the significance of culture, and the authority of Scripture.

APPLYING PRINCIPLES

God's Word is not a minutely detailed code of practice for the Christian. Issues confront us today which may not be directly dealt with in the Bible. For example, new scientific techniques have been developed in the field of childbirth which raise questions of medical ethics; new social and political structures have emerged which were unknown in the first century. Even in the pages of the New Testament, problems and issues are dealt with because they arose in particular situations encountered by the apostles—not because they exhaust all the possible situations envisaged by the inspired writers. In these senses we can readily accept that there are 'omissions' in Scripture, without in any way questioning the sufficiency of God's Word. Indeed, to extend the quotation from the Westminster Confession given a moment ago, we are speaking consistently with the assertion that

> The whole counsel of God, concerning all things necessary for His own glory, man's salvation, faith, and life, is either expressly set down in Scripture, or **by good and necessary consequence may be deduced from Scripture.**
>
> Chapter 1, *vi*

How, then, are we to apply the teaching of God's Word to our own situation and society? When we come to the Bible's teaching on social issues, we are given 'a set of broad guiding principles with sample applications to set us going . . . [that] are not so much models for mechanical imitation as cartoons of required attitudes' (J. I. Packer).[2] The much misunderstood 'Golden Rule' — 'In everything, do to others what you would have them do to you, for this sums up the Law and the Prophets' (Matt. 7:12)—is one of the aids that Scripture gives us in applying principles. So also is the teaching about the image of God in man, and its implications, which we discussed in the opening chapter. Again, Scripture very often suggests that the attitude of imitating Christ provides a key to dealing with social and personal problems (e.g. 1 Pet. 1:16; 2:13— 3:7). While recognizing that there will be conscientious differences of opinion (e.g. Acts 15:36-41), the Christian is to press forward, praying for the illumination of the Holy Spirit and guided by the twin motives of love to God and to our neighbour.

There are, however, a number of signposts and warnings that need to be erected. There is a tendency in some recent evangelical writing to place altogether too much weight on this distinction between principles and their application. The line of reasoning goes something like this. Scripture contains both general principles and some applications of those principles. However, the applications are culture-bound—not simply in those cases where culturally obsolete practices are evident (in Western society, examples of such practices would include foot-washing, meat offered to idols, etc.), but in every case of ethical teaching. These applications were relevant to their time, but, as we live in a fundamentally different culture, we are to start again with the principles and not be governed by the applications found in Scripture.

The Bible's teaching on capital punishment provides an example. Taking general principles like the dignity of man and the possibility of divine forgiveness, some evangelical writers argue that while 'literalistic' interpretations of certain passages give support to capital punishment, the church's development of general biblical principles allows us to reject capital punishment today. The implication is that we can consign to obsolescence the Bible's explicit teaching on the subject.

There are several difficulties and dangers with this approach. *First*, it runs the risk of interpreting the plain in the light of the obscure or uncertain. For example, writing about Priscilla's ministry, Howard Marshall poses the question of 'how one harmonises the prohibition of 1 Timothy 2' (i.e. on women exercising a teaching ministry to men) 'with the implicit [sic] principles elsewhere in the New Testament.'[3] *Secondly,* the procedure becomes a subjective exercise, too easily reflecting the

25

bias of the interpreter. How do we know that an abstract principle drawn from a particular biblical account is correct? *Thirdly*, there is a grave danger that the interpreter can sidestep the Bible's own application of general principles when they are not to his liking, and hence the message of the text is evaded. *Finally*, in practice, the reliance on general, implicit principles sometimes seems to be a way of opening up other sources of authority apart from the written Word. Marshall's writing again serves to illustrate this problem, in that he appears to regard Scripture as containing a mixture of divine revelation, application of principles found elsewhere in Scripture, appeal to natural law, common sense and custom, etc.[4] If Scripture contains such a mishmash, might not our own approach to social issues be based on similar grounds?

On this basis how can Scripture be said to be clear and comprehensible? How can the ordinary Christian reach any degree of certainty about the teaching of Scripture, without expert help to disentangle the threads and achieve an understanding of the text acceptable to the modern interpreter?

The Christian needs to insist that biblical applications of ethical principles were themselves directed by the Holy Spirit, and hence are of a fundamentally different status from our own applications of biblical principles. This remains true, however difficult we find it to cope with them (e.g. Old Testament teaching on genocide), and however much we still rightly insist on our obligation to reapply biblical principles.

THE TWO TESTAMENTS

To understand and obey New Testament teaching on social ethics may seem difficult. But what about the Old Testament teaching? Most of us would probably agree that Old Testament social ethics cannot be transferred in a simple way to our society. Indeed, when attempts are made to do this, we rapidly find ourselves arguing for strange positions. If we think, as some Christians do, that the social and political laws of the Old Testament remain valid, we may find ourselves arguing that it is a sign of tyrannical rule when a government takes 10 per cent or more of a citizen's income in taxes, defending our position on the grounds that Samuel warned that a king would take a tenth of their crops and flocks (1 Sam. 8:15,17). Furthermore, we may consider that a property tax is a sign of a denial of the lordship of the triune God, because the Old Testament taught tithing![5] On this view of things, Value Added Tax (at 10 per cent, of course) is thoroughly biblical, whereas the annual rates bill would gravely trouble our consciences!

Clearly we must allow for discontinuity between the two Testaments, or our Christian witness will be in a strait-jacket of rigid legalism. Does this mean, then, that Old and New Testament teaching on social issues are basically different? Is Old Testament teaching on polygamy, divorce, war, the death penalty, the discipline of disobedient children and so on, a relic of the old covenant which has no relevance today?

Perhaps the most important single statement on the relationship of the two Testaments came from the lips of our Lord, when He announced: 'Do not think that I have come to abolish the Law or the Prophets; I have not come to abolish them but to fulfil them' (Matt. 5:17). What does this statement mean for us?

First, Christ's coming does not destroy or abolish Old Testament teaching on social ethics. The entire Old Testament possesses continuing validity as the Word of God. But what does this mean in practice? In *Reactivating the Extended Family* Michael Schluter and Roy Clements have done much to formulate a biblical approach to this question.

They argue that the Old Testament is addressing a different audience from that found in the New. The New Testament is written to individual disciples, and represents the full standard that God requires of Christians, and by which they will be judged (e.g. Matt. 5—7). Old Testament law, on the other hand, is law for society as a whole, for the unregenerate as well as the regenerate, and in the main is to be enforced by society. It takes into account man's evil nature (cf. Matt. 19:8) and is a compromise or second-best solution, which seeks to restrain rather than eradicate evil. In this sense, the Old Testament is a model not only for God's people, but also for God's dealings with society. Over against the procedure of deriving general principles and reclothing them in twentieth century garb, these writers regard the OT Law as a normative *'model'* of political economy, and the history of Israel as the record of the implementation of that model in a particular historical context.[6]

The advantage of this approach is that the Old Testament is viewed as a whole. This enables us to see the apparently harsh Old Testament laws relating to genocide, punishment of disobedient children and so on in their proper context.

We may not wish to go all the way with Schluter and Clements. In saying that the Old Testament law is for unregenerate society as a whole, I think they overstate the distinction between law and gospel. Clearly, much of the Old Testament law is given to people in covenant with God, and we are running the risk of legalism if we seek to apply to mankind generally principles which God gave to

27

people who acknowledged His authority. However, these writers, and others like Chris Wright,[7] illustrate the way in which we should take note of the Old Testament as well as the New.

Our reading of the Old Testament should not be restricted to the law. People like Joseph, Daniel, Ezra, Nehemiah, Mordecai and Esther all illustrate what we may expect of God's people living under governments which do not acknowledge God.

But, secondly, Christ's words in Matthew 5:17 also emphasize that He 'fulfilled' the law. He did not simply affirm the law's validity, but added a new revelation without which the Old Testament is incomplete. Throughout chapter 5 of Matthew, Christ is spelling out the full implications of the commandments— commandments which prove more comprehensive, radical and exacting than they had ever supposed. The Jews with their scribal interpretations had exalted what God intended as temporary commandments (e.g. Deut. 24:1) to the status of the permanent. Christ fulfilled the law in the sense that He set aside the temporary and underlined the permanent (cf. Matt. 19:1-10). If we ask why God, in His longsuffering, tolerated certain practices in the Old Testament which were against His revealed will, the answer is that we do not fully know. But God's revelation was progressive, and, on the principle enunciated by Christ (Luke 12:48), a lesser punishment falls on those Old Testament violations of His revealed will. An example of ways in which Old Testament teaching has a bearing on social issues is found in the chapter on social welfare, where we discuss the significance for our own day of God's judgments on the nations surrounding Israel.

THE SIGNIFICANCE OF CULTURE

Were we to visit a church for the first time and meet a couple in the congregation, we would expect either the wife or the husband to introduce their partner. They would probably introduce themselves using their Christian name. If we were to stay for the service, we would assume that the husband and wife would sit together, perhaps with their children near to them. Their special relationship would be 'signalled' to us by physical proximity, by occasional smiles (or looks of annoyance!) or by an exchange of glances. If we were invited to their house, we would expect to talk informally with their children, and so on. For us, these are all obvious parts of normal life. And yet in some parts of the world—e.g. among the churches of Central Africa—there would be little or nothing of this behaviour, and it would be regarded as neither 'obvious' nor 'normal'. Men and women would probably sit on separate sides of the church, sons remaining with their fathers and daughters with their mothers. Christian names would not be used, perhaps not even in conversation between husband and wife; physical contact, even an innocuous holding of hands, would be regarded with acute embarrassment.

This very simple illustration serves to remind us that much which we regard as fixed, permanent and natural is, in reality, part of our culture. To others it is none of these things.

We have already observed that arguments about the need for reapplying biblical principles in the twentieth century are often grounded on a belief that biblical applications were worked out in terms of cultures fundamentally different from our own. For our obedience to the Word of God to be faithful, it has been said that we need patterns of behaviour which have what is sometimes called a 'dynamic equivalence' to biblical patterns, rather than a literal, mechanical imitation.

Perhaps, before we proceed, a rough definition of the term 'culture' is necessary. It denotes the system of beliefs, values and customs of a society, tribe or community, and the institutions which give expression to those beliefs, values and customs and normally help to bind a society together. (Such institutions include the legal system, schools, churches and families.) Christian preoccupation with culture came to the fore with the rapid growth of the social sciences from the 1960s onwards. Culture is an issue for the Christian from two viewpoints: first, the culture of the Bible reader today and, second, the cultures of the Bible.

I should make clear that I think that cultural issues are a much overrated problem in Christian thinking at the present time. This often stems from having too high a regard for present-day cultures. Cultural arguments are in danger of being adopted as an escape route when the teaching of Scripture is found to be uncomfortable. Take this recent instance of a comment on Peter's command to wives: 'In the same way be submissive to your husbands so that, if any of them do not believe the word, they may be won over without talk by the behaviour of their wives' (1 Pet. 3:1). 'It must be emphasised', we are told, 'that the restriction on verbal witness to their husbands was probably culturally based' (Howard Marshall).[8] This is an unnecessary conclusion. The clear implication of Peter's words is not that verbal witness was inappropriate, but that such witness had already taken place and been rejected ('if any of them do not believe the word'). In Peter's supporting argument in the following verses there is no hint of a culturally based justification for his words.

Nevertheless, culture—both the Bible's and ours—*is* important.

29

Indeed, unless we think that all of Scripture teaching is principle, we are forced to establish guidelines that will enable us to recognize the ways in which God requires our obedience in today's world. The reader's anxiety may rise at this point. Is not this almost like suggesting that Scripture is unclear or even inadequate? Where is the lucidity of God's Word of which we spoke earlier? What we mean by this statement is that we are all to some extent conditioned by the cultural environment in which we live, and that this tends to determine what we are able to 'see' in Scripture:

> It is not that God's Word is unclear in itself, nor that its meaning is captive to any culture. The problem lies rather within our minds as we read . . . It is our sin, as it comes to expression in our various cultural assumptions and tries to find justification in them, which often blinds our eyes to what God wants us to see in His Word.
>
> J. Stott[9]

In the words of the apostle Paul, 'Now we see but a poor reflection' (1 Cor. 13:12).

We have much to learn from the attitudes of the biblical writers to culture, and this in turn should shape our own attitude. The Word of God repeatedly emphasizes the transience of this present age and culture.[10] 'Here we have no continuing city' (Heb. 13:14, AV), and 'this world in its present form is passing away'. Hence,

> From now on those who have wives should live as if they had none; those who mourn, as if they did not; those who are happy, as if they were not; those who buy something, as if it were not theirs to keep; those who use the things of the world, as if not engrossed in them.
>
> 1 Corinthians 7:29-31

In his obedience to the call to leave his country, his people and his father's household (Gen. 12:1), Abraham is a spiritual pattern for us all. The Christian is given a certain amount of cultural freedom. Matters of cultural indifference should not be made binding (cf. Rom. 14:5-8; Col. 2:16). David Smith has said of Abraham that 'while remaining a man in time and history, he possesses a critical perspective on his own time and culture. The Word of God reaches us via our own culture, yet contains a judgment on that culture. Thus, the line between good and evil does not run *between* cultures but *through* every culture.'[11]

The Bible is never indifferent to culture. It is often through the hearer's own culture that the gospel makes an initial point of contact. At the same time, the Bible is frequently 'culturally imperialistic' (Zink), seeming initially to accommodate to the

30

culture of the time, but then subverting it. Thus, Paul preaches to the Athenians in terms of their altar to an unknown god, and even quotes their own writers, before setting this in the context of the nature of God and the message of the resurrection (Acts 17).

We can make contact with our own culture in a similar way. In modern music, for example, there is much that is sensual, hedonistic and thoroughly pagan. However, where can we find a sharper realization of the emptiness of much twentieth-century culture than in some modern music? Paul Simon's songs, from his earliest albums to the most recent *Graceland*, are a clear example.

'Let us be lovers. We'll marry our fortunes together.
I've got some real estate here in my bag.'
So we bought a pack of cigarettes,
And Mrs Wagner's pies,
And walked off to look for America.
'Kathy,' I said, as we boarded a Greyhound in Pittsburgh,
'Michigan seems like a dream to me now.
It took me four days to hitchhike from Saginaw.
I've come to look for America.'
Laughing on the bus, playing games with the faces,
She said the man in the gabardine suit was a spy.
I said, 'Be careful, his bowtie is really a camera.'

'Toss me a cigarette, I think there's one in my raincoat.'
'We smoked the last one an hour ago.'
So I looked at the scenery,
She read her magazine;
And the moon rose over an open field.
'Kathy, I'm lost', I said, though I knew she was sleeping.
'I'm empty and aching and I don't know why.'
Counting the cars on the New Jersey Turnpike.
They've all come to look for America,
All come to look for America.

Paul Simon, 'America' (1968)

By word and life the Christian is to speak an all-pervading gospel into a Christless twentieth-century culture. He is to use every God-given handhold on the consciences of people.

How then are we to distinguish cultural expressions from abiding principles? The question is a big one. All we can do here is suggest a few straightforward guides. *First*, we are to observe the way the Bible itself seeks to justify a given practice. If Scripture appeals to permanent truths to justify a practice (e.g. creation, the image of God in man, Christ's person or work), then we can be sure that a general principle is involved. *Secondly*, if there are cultural practices which are obviously strange to us (e.g. meat offered to idols, foot-washing, slavery and, I would suggest, veiling), then a

31

reapplication of Scripture is called for. Foot-washing is an obvious and simple example to which reference is often made. The principle involved may perhaps be expressed as follows: we should be ready to serve one another in a way that demonstrates mutual love and an absence of social hierarchy among God's people. There are many ways in which this may find expression. In Western cultures, washing the dinner dishes for your host is only one example. *Thirdly*, we must beware of dogmatism, being willing to admit ignorance and careful not to over-interpret the text. There are aspects of the teaching about head-covering, for example, which are difficult. What did Paul mean when he said that a woman ought to have a sign of authority on her head 'because of the angels', or that 'the very nature of things' teaches that it is a disgrace for a man to have long hair, but a glory for the woman? *Finally*, in applying the Word of God to our own culture, 'It is not always noticed that God provides much of the answer to this perplexity in the person of the preacher, who is called to be a living advertisement for the relevance and power of what he proclaims' (J. I. Packer).[12]

Not all situations are as straightforward. For instance, food offered to idols, veiling, polygamy and servants may all be culturally distant from most British families. However, in many situations elsewhere in the world one or more of these topics is a live issue for the Christian. Furthermore, Scripture teaching intertwines principle and cultural application. Usually, this is readily evident and causes no difficulty to the reader. Take the following:

> I also want women to dress modestly, with decency and propriety, not with braided hair or gold or pearls or expensive clothes, but with good deeds, appropriate for women who profess to worship God.
>
> 1 Timothy 2:9-10

Paul is giving instructions on worship in a much discussed passage which is taken up elsewhere in this book by Elizabeth Catherwood. The point we need to notice here is that the apostle is laying down ethical principles—modesty, decency, propriety and good deeds—which are not at all limited to a given culture. However, his applications apply to the cultural context in which he writes. It would appear, for example, that 'braided hair' referred to certain contemporary hair styles which had moral implications.

Some writers would go further than this, suggesting that when Paul speaks of the role of women in worship, or of slavery and other topics, his whole approach is governed by his own day. If he were writing for today, they argue, he would write differently. What is required of us, therefore, is to be faithful to the 'genius' or 'central thrust' of his teaching. For example, we live in a day unlike Paul's day, when women have been educated, and for them to remain silent today would cause as much offence as their speaking out would have done in Paul's day.

However, as the passage proceeds (1 Tim. 2:9-15), Paul appears to make no reference to cultural factors in explaining his position. Even though we may find it difficult at first to understand the force of his argument ('Adam was formed first . . . And Adam was not the one deceived . . . But women will be saved [NIV margin] through childbearing . . .'), there is no evidence that a different cultural context would have altered Paul's answer. Moreover, the morality of this whole approach is highly dubious. Are we saying that, if Paul were alive today, he would justify keeping women out of positions of authority in some Third World churches, while teaching different standards in the West? The possibility is unthinkable!

The argument we have just considered does at least do Paul the favour of assuming that he knew what he was saying! Some writers, evangelicals among them, take a further step and claim that Paul's views on this matter and others were hangovers of rabbinical teaching. Paul, in other words, is sub-Christian and not to be followed.

When Paul, speaking about worship to the Corinthians, says that women 'are not allowed to speak, but must be in submission, as the Law says' (1 Cor. 14:34), Joyce Baldwin reasons that the apostle was referring to the Jewish law of his day. Paul was simply appealing to current practice, to convince his contemporaries. 'If a rabbinic argument suited his purpose Paul felt free to use it.'[13] Hence, we should not infer from Paul's teaching that it necessarily applies in every respect today.

The argument has thus moved on to different ground. It is no longer a case of how we apply Paul's principles, but whether Paul's principles have the authority of inspired Scripture at all. It is the authority of Scripture itself which is under debate.

We need to affirm that God's unchanging Word speaks authoritatively to cultural behaviour. It addresses some aspects of it that, in the West at least, have passed away (e.g. slavery); it also addresses cultures that we are free to change (e.g. forms of government); and it has important things to say about the culture that God requires us to maintain (e.g. forms of authority in church and family).[14]

33

An example may help at this point. How are we to understand Paul's teaching on the relationship between the Christian and the state in Romans 13? The range of interpretations currently on offer shows clearly that the Bible's teaching on social issues cannot be considered without immediately raising questions about the interpretation and authority of the Word of God. Paul's words are familiar:

> Everyone must submit himself to the governing authorities, for there is no authority except that which God has established. The authorities that exist have been established by God. Consequently he who rebels against the authority is rebelling against what God has instituted, and those who do so will bring judgment on themselves. For rulers hold no terror for those who do right, but for those who do wrong. Do you want to be free from fear of the one in authority? Then do what is right and he will commend you. For he is God's servant to do you good. But if you do wrong, be afraid, for he does not bear the sword for nothing. He is God's servant, an agent of wrath to bring punishment on the wrongdoer.
>
> Romans 13:1-4

There are three broad views on this passage. The traditional view, perhaps held by many readers of this chapter, is that all governments are to be accepted as God's servants. Calvin expresses it clearly. While Paul 'speaks here of the true . . . duty of the magistrate' from which many degenerate, 'yet the obedience due to princes ought to be rendered to them.' Wicked rulers are a scourge sent by the Lord to punish the sins of the people. In addition, 'princes do never so far abuse their power . . . that they do not retain in their tyranny some kind of just government: there can be no tyranny which does not in some respects assist in consolidating the society of men.'

This position has increasingly come under fire. Is Calvin right in saying that all tyrannies confer some degree of social benefit? And is he going too far in implying that wicked rulers are (always?) a scourge sent by God?

A view that is opposite in almost every respect to Calvin's has been put forward by Wilmer. His fundamental position is that Paul's prescription is unworkable and has proved 'a momentously influential text which many have taken to endorse states like Nero's and Hitler's.' Paul, he reasons, is claiming that government 'puts no obstacles or disincentives in the way of doing good'—a position which 'does not describe any state we know or might make.' For example, democracy, because it institutionalizes opposition, 'is not compatible with Romans 13:3'. He concludes: 'The history of the development of our democratic, parliamentary state is also the history of a people's experience of the political unworkability of Romans 13 and of their attempts to cope with its consequences.'[15]

This position illustrates a disturbingly cavalier attitude to Scripture from someone who writes as an evangelical. He appears ready to acknowledge that Paul may have believed he was writing 'theologically', but he rejects Paul's solution as entirely unworkable and damaging.

A very different approach has been suggested by Bruce Kaye. The essence of his position is that Romans 13 applies only to *just* governments. Rather than making a point of universal application, Paul is referring to the particular authorities of his day. Writing in a period of settled government, Paul is urging submission to *those* authorities. Rulers *at that point in time* held 'no terror for those who do right' (v.3). Kaye starts from the problem that Paul's statement in verses 3 and 4 ('rulers hold no terror for those who do right, but for those who do wrong . . .') appears to him 'manifestly not true' if construed as a general statement. Paul is approving the authorities *because* they commend good and are a terror to those who do wrong.[16]

What is our response to this viewpoint? Unlike Wilmer, Kaye is clearly committed to the text of Scripture as it stands. Furthermore, his approach pushes us afresh to renewed study of what the Word of God actually says and means. My hesitations are twofold. Paul does appear to be saying *more* than Kaye suggests. The natural sense of Paul's language is to understand it in universal terms (e.g. 'there is no authority except that which God has established', v.1). Second, there is biblical guidance elsewhere which is couched in very similar terms (e.g. 1 Pet. 2:13-14), but which is certainly not written to those who were enjoying just government.

We have given a brief survey of Christian comment on Romans 13, not because we think it answers the questions Christians ought to consider regarding their relationship to the state, but because it provides, almost as a case study, an illustration of the variety of approaches to applying Scripture to social issues. Calvin represents the historical, Reformed perspective; Kaye illustrates just one example of exegesis that seeks to take the contemporary cultural context into account in a thoroughgoing fashion; Wilmer, in what is admittedly a rather extreme example, represents a disturbing tendency to play fast and loose with the revealed Word of God. It may be possible to understand and apply Romans 13 and 1 Peter 2 by recognizing that the state is God's servant, commissioned and sent by God Himself 'to punish those who do wrong and to commend those who do right' (1 Pet. 2:14). In revealing how governments ought to function, however, God has also provided criteria by which the performance of governments (and, by analogy, that of parents, husbands, slave-owners, etc.) could be judged. The same criteria are applicable today.[17]

We started this chapter with the twin assertions that Scripture has something relevant to say on the subject of social issues, and that as evangelical Christians we are bound by the authority of Scripture. Yet, necessary as these convictions are, we have seen that they are broad enough to include too wide a range of views. To say Scripture is relevant is not to say much. We need to define the authority of God's Word in such a way that it excludes the possibility that the apostles were wittingly or unwittingly purveying rabbinical views, or that Scripture contains ethical inconsistencies that jeopardize the application of the New Testament to our own situation.

Furthermore, we have argued in the opening chapter that the teaching of Scripture is binding in matters such as the organization and government of the local church. This is not to say that all our problems are immediately solved by this principle, but it gives the Christian a cast of mind, a set of assumptions, which create in him an expectancy that what the New Testament has to say about social issues and the local church will shed considerable light on our endeavours to live as salt and light in an unbelieving world.

NOTES

1 J. Murray, 'The Finality and Sufficiency of Scripture', in *Collected Writings, I: The Claims of Truth* (Banner of Truth, 1976), p.22.
2 J. I. Packer, 'Conscience, Choice and Character, in *Law, Morality and the Bible*, ed. by B. N. Kaye and G. J. Wenham (Inter-Varsity Press, 1978), p.180.
3 I. H. Marshall, 'The Role of Women in the Church', in *The Role of Women*, ed. by S. Lees (Inter-Varsity Press, 1984), p.153.
4 I. H. Marshall, 'Using the Bible in Ethics', in *Essays in Evangelical Social Ethics*, ed. by D. F. Wright (Paternoster, n.d.), p.41.
5 R. J. Rushdoony argues along these lines. For a simple example, see pages 47-50 of his *Bread Upon the Waters* (Cornerstone Publishers, 1974).
6 M. Schluter and R. Clements, *Reactivating the Extended Family: From Biblical Norms to Public Policy in Britain* (Jubilee Centre, 1986), p.32.
7 C. J. H. Wright, *Living as the People of God* (Inter-Varsity Press, 1983).
8 I. H. Marshall, *The Role of Women*, p.183.
9 *Evangelism and Social Responsibility*: The Lausanne Conference Report (Paternoster, 1982), pp.10-11.

10 I am indebted here to a lecture by David Zink of L'Abri Fellowship in Massachusetts on *Interpreting the 'Culturally Relative' in Scripture.*

11 D. Smith, 'The Bible and Culture', *Christian Arena*, 39.4 (1986).

12 J. I. Packer, 'Why Preach?' in *Preaching*, ed. by S. T. Logan (Evangelical Press, 1986), p.17.

13 J. Baldwin, 'Women's Ministry — A New Look at the Biblical Texts', in *The Role of Women*, ed. by S. Lees (Inter-Varsity Press, 1984), p.165.

14 Hurley has helpfully argued the way in which Scripture itself makes this three-fold distinction in *Man and Woman in Biblical Perspective* (Inter-Varsity Press, 1981), pp.157-61.

15 H. Wilmer, 'Towards a Theology of the State', in *Essays in Evangelical Social Ethics*, ed. by D. Wright (Paternoster, n.d.), pp.88-9.

16 B. N. Kaye 'The New Testament and Social Order' in *Law, Morality and the Bible* (Inter-Varsity Press, 1978), pp.104-8.

17 Donald MacLeod reasons along similar lines in a later chapter of this book. On Romans 13 he states: 'Paul's immediate concern . . . is to lay down the basis of obedience to the state. But the principles he sets forth also provide a basis for criticism of the state.'

QUESTIONS FOR DISCUSSION

a) Concentrating on one of the subjects dealt with in the second part of this book, how may we apply the teaching of Scripture in the light of the issues raised in this chapter?

b) Consider in detail at least one of the Old Testament characters mentioned on page 28. What do we learn about the possibilities for Christian social action in a mixed society?

FURTHER READING

There is increasing need for a careful discussion of the questions touched on in this chapter. Marshall has provided one of the few examinations of these issues, and his work ought to be read. We have, however, indicated in this chapter a number of reservations about the arguments he puts forward. J. I. Packer writes helpfully about applying biblical principles in his chapter 'Conscience, Choice and Character' in *Law, Morality and the Bible* edited by Kaye and Wenham (Inter-Varsity Press, 1978). Stonehouse's discussion of Matthew 5:17 in *The Witness of Matthew and Mark to Christ* (Baker, 1979) is a useful comment on the relation of the two Testaments. D. Martyn Lloyd-Jones takes a similar approach in his excellent *Studies in the Sermon on the Mount* (Inter-Varsity Press, 1959). I have already mentioned Michael Schluter's and Roy Clements' discussion in *Reactivating the Extended Family* (Jubilee Centre, 1986), and Chris Wright's book on Old Testament ethics, *Living as the People of God* (Inter-Varsity Press, 1983), should also be consulted. Bruce Kaye has written in the series of Grove booklets on ethics on *Using the Bible in Ethics* (Grove Books, 1976). On the significance of culture, a major example of an attempt to study the Word of God in the light of the cultures of biblical authors is Jim Hurley's *Man and Woman in Biblical Perspective* (Inter-Varsity Press, 1981).

3

Social Issues and the Local Church

OLIVER R. BARCLAY

We must start by trying to see social issues in a biblical perspective. For this purpose I want to take two key chapters in the Epistle to the Romans (Romans 12 and 13) as an example. The train of thought runs like this.

First, the basis of everything lies in the mercies of God (12:1). The whole sweep of the gospel outlined in the first eleven chapters of Romans is in view here. We cannot jump straight into social issues without remembering that the gospel is the foundation of the whole life of the Christian and of the church. In the book of Romans it is the gospel that occupies the major place.

Nevertheless, the mercies of God lead us not only to worship and to thanksgiving (v.1) but also to a renewed mind (v.2). That is to say, the gospel has consequences for our whole outlook, our priorities, and our attitudes to ourselves, our neighbours, our church, *and our society*. It must not stop with inward experiences, though it starts there with the regenerating work of the Holy Spirit. This new outlook begins with a new humility about ourselves: 'Do not think of yourself more highly than you ought' (v.3). The gospel brings us down to the dust, but then it lifts us up again: 'but rather think of yourself with sober judgment, in accordance with the measure of faith God has given you . . . We have different gifts, according to the grace given us' (vv.3-6). God has tasks for His children in the world. They are not all the same. Some are evangelists, or pastors and teachers, while others are housewives, schoolmasters, policemen and social workers. Not every person is gifted for active involvement in social affairs, and those who are are unlikely to be also gifted for church ministry. In the local churches there should be a variety of functions ('members do not all have the same function', v.4). No one should propose that all Christians must be deeply involved in social issues, but, as I hope to

39

show, some ought to be as a matter of God's gift and calling. There is something wrong if no one is using God-given gifts to influence the life of society for good.

Next, however, Paul goes on to stress that the results of a proper outworking of the varied gifts that God has given are all part of the development of a life of love ('Let love be genuine', v.9 RSV). The rest of the chapter can be seen as an outworking of this theme of the practice of love, which is an essential foundation aspect of that true sanctification which springs from the gospel. Social involvement is not pre-evangelism. It is post-evangelism—an aspect of sanctification—the outworking of love. That is to say, we do not do it to impress the world or prepare their minds for the gospel, though the consistent Christian life may of course help here. We do it rather in obedience to God's command to live out a life of love for all men, and to be salt and light where He has put us. In any case, much social action will not impress the unregenerate at all; it may initially antagonize them, especially if we ask for greater righteousness. (Sunday legislation, pornography and similar issues illustrate this well.) But it is what may be demanded of us (depending on our gifts) by way of obedience to the moral claims of the Scriptures. Indeed, it is difficult to see how any Christian can refuse to be at least concerned and to pray about the needs of good order in society, as I hope to show.

Romans 13 follows the same pattern. The first seven verses set out the doctrine of the state (it is part of the renewed mind of 12:2 to have such a doctrinal view). There is no mention of love there; all is authority, justice and wrath. But then verses 8-10 bring us back to love. The church is to live in love within the order of society that God has ordained. The end of chapter 12 forms the preamble to chapter 13, though this is obscured by the chapter division. The train of thought is as follows: 'Repay no one evil for evil . . . never avenge yourselves, but leave it to the *wrath* of God' (12:17,19 RSV). The state is then described as the means that God has appointed for that task. The governing authority is 'the servant of God to execute his *wrath* on the wrongdoer' (13:4 RSV). That is to say, the state is God's minister of wrath, while the Christian in his personal capacity is to be the minister of God's love and mercy.

What that life of love is like is then described, perhaps to our surprise, in terms of the Ten Commandments (13:8-10). Love is not merely emotion; it has a definite biblical 'shape'. In Ephesians 4—6 Paul again sets out the Christian life in terms of these commandments, following very closely the exposition given by our Lord in the Sermon on the Mount. (The relationship between Ephesians and Matthew 5 makes a very instructive study.) So, even though the commandments were given originally under the old covenant, we have powerful biblical precedent for setting out the duties of the Christian life in this framework. To live a life of love can, therefore, be expressed in terms of living out the Ten Commandments.

Romans 12 and 13, then, set our concern for society firstly in the context of our response to the gospel and, secondly, in the context of the life of love of which it is a part. This setting is essential if we are to see it rightly in relation to our other Christian responsibilities.

DOES GOD CARE ABOUT GOOD ORDER IN SOCIETY?

We often forget that most of the New Testament epistles lead us in the same way as Romans *from* the gospel *to* the outworking of the Christian life in the daily work and varied responsibilities of Christians. Some Christians have interpreted this to mean that we need not be interested in the good order of society or in the relative improvements in material and social conditions, but give our minds only to the gospel and to personal piety. But why then does Romans 13 give us a doctrine of the state which tells us what the state should do and that God cares for good government? Why does it place that in the middle of teaching about the Christian life of love? I suggest that this is because a right view of the state is needed if we are to live in love. One aspect of love will be seen in our response to the proper demands and role of the state, and in doing our best to ensure that the state plays its part in supporting justice and righteousness for others. That, according to this passage, is what God intends and wishes it to do. Let us consider other passages which emphasize the same thing.

In Matthew 5:45-48, we are told that God 'causes his sun to rise on the evil and the good, and sends rain on the righteous and the unrighteous', and that we are to imitate Him in this. The pattern of God's blessings to men includes helping the totally unresponsive and doing good to them on a human and material level.

Jesus' own ministry also followed this pattern. He healed ten lepers, when He probably knew that only one would even say thank you. He fed the four thousand because, according to Matthew 15:32, He was concerned that otherwise they would faint on the way to get food. On another occasion it is said that He 'healed them all', and it is quite clear that they did not all become believers. He raised the widow of Nain's son out of pure pity, as far as we can tell.

41

We find the same emphasis in the New Testament epistles. We are to pray for good government, that will enable us to live in peace (1 Tim. 2:1-2). We are also to do good to all men (Gal. 6:10). The Christian is to care for the physical needs of his older relatives (1 Tim. 5:8) and live a life that is 'profitable to men' (Tit. 3:8 RSV).

The Old Testament also shows repeatedly that God cares enormously, giving instructions for the good order, health and well-being of a very mixed society, and even also for pagan societies. So God *does* care, and His generosity and goodness towards us are meant to bring us to repentance (Rom. 2:4). Only when we fail to respond to His love does God turn to judgment. It is not God's plan that we should be as miserable as possible so that we may look for heavenly things. His first witness to us is in the manifold goodness of the creation, so that we may be grateful. He wants us to enjoy health and to experience human and social well-being.

Finally, how do we bring glory to God in the world? According to Matthew 5:13-16, we do this by living out our faith: 'Let your light shine before men, that they may see your *good deeds* and praise your Father in heaven' (v.16). We are to be salt and light in *that* sense, and not only in the sense of preaching the gospel. So we are to be a people who 'do good to *all people*, especially to those who belong to the family of believers' (Gal. 6:10). We are therefore to be like parents who care for their children. Above all, we care for their spiritual good, but we also care for their physical and mental health and would be deeply ashamed if we failed to do our part at all levels. That is what love does. We do not starve our children so that they may be miserable and hope for heaven! Neither does God, though when all else fails He turns to judgment. Isaiah 1:18-20 illustrates this: '"Come now, let us reason together," says the Lord. "Though your sins are like scarlet, they shall be as white as snow . . . but if you resist and rebel, you will be devoured by the sword".'

GOD'S IDEALS FOR A FALLEN WORLD

God's ultimate ideals for society are the creation ideals. Thus, in Matthew 19 when Jesus is asked about divorce, He goes back to creation. The ideals of the perfect world and of the kingdom of God must always be before us. We are not to regard anything less as an acceptable ultimate ideal. Nevertheless, ours is a fallen world and that ideal is not a goal that sinful men can realize. This is why Moses in a mixed society regulated (and limited) divorce 'because of the hardness of your hearts' (Matt. 19:8 AV). For the same

42

reason Jesus Himself allowed divorce for the Christian in one situation where there is irreversible evil, although this is not the kingdom ideal (Matt. 5:32 and 19:9). Our practical aim for society may often have to be well below the kingdom ideal, and this realizable aim can be called the 'practical ideal for a fallen world'.

The problem in a fallen world is of course, first of all, fallen people. This means that in the actual world as we have it (and even in the actual church) there must be checks and balances that restrain evil and encourage good, and limit what evil people can do. Many of the provisions of the Old Testament, even for a covenanted people, are controls of this sort that will be unnecessary in heaven, and some, but not all, should be unnecessary in the church. Cities of refuge, law courts, armies, etc., are all to pass away in the ultimate ideal, but they or their equivalents are needed because of sin. The Christian should share the Old Testament concern for good order and good structures in society if we are to have any measure of peace. According to the Bible, we are to pray for peace (1 Tim. 2) and also to pay for it (Rom. 13), though both these passages recognize that we do not go directly to seek peace, but we have to deal with those things that make it difficult to obtain. The Bible, therefore, does not tell us to do away with law courts, but to make sure that they are justly administered; it does not tell us to do away with private property, but to control its likely abuses. There is, therefore, in the Bible a whole range of what we may call a kind of 'interim ethics' for a fallen world, which will be unnecessary when the kingdom of God is fulfilled.

The fallen state of man, however, has another consequence. We are unable to create ideal structures. No order of society is perfect. The Old Testament order was the best possible one for that society, but it still could not altogether eliminate injustice, bribery, etc. The pathetic confidence of some Christians and secular idealists that if only we could scrap the present structures (whether capitalist, socialist, liberal, or whatever), we could arrive at a just society, is an illusion. Even a return to the Old Testament order with its jubilee provisions etc. would not solve the problems. We are stuck with a world in which, first of all, sinful people will abuse whatever social order we create, and in which, secondly, no social order is itself perfect. We are not yet in heaven. The most we can say of any social structure is that in the light of Scripture we believe it is the best that can be achieved at the moment, although it will create some injustices and have other imperfections. Good laws often create very hard cases. Meanwhile, whatever our politics may be, we will be trying to improve the order we have, so that there may be a greater degree of conformity to the will of God.

There is today much talk of 'sinful' structures in society. I believe this is dangerous language for several reasons, not least because sin is something of which you are guilty and of which you must repent. To many people this terminology implies that what you have to do is to repent of the present 'sinful' structures and all will be well. In fact, however, the structures are rarely the result of deliberate sin, but they *and any structure we put in their place* will, in a fallen world, be imperfect, tainted by evil (not personal sin), and therefore in principle capable of a further measure of improvement or deterioration. Some Christians have lapsed into a sort of utopianism, either because they believe we can have heaven (or the kingdom of heaven) here on earth, or because they believe that if only we repented of the evils of our society, we could have another structure that will be free of evil. In a fallen world all structures have some evil in them. Even the worst government is in some ways better than anarchy, and bad government must be improved and its evils reduced. As has often been said, if you think you have found the perfect church, then you had better not join it or it will immediately become imperfect! If this is true of the church, how much more must it be said of society! The fact is that we are neither in hell nor in heaven, and even in the church men are neither devils nor angels. This, however, must not prevent us from trying to improve what we have. In heaven there will be no need to improve things; in hell there will be no hope; but on earth even unregenerate men have still a moral sense (Rom. 2) and can be awakened to seek some improvement in the society we have.

If it is objected that Christians are too few to have much influence, then church history shows that this is not necessarily so. Many of the very substantial social reforms of the early nineteenth century were led by evangelical Christians who, although they were quite a small number, found a considerable body of non-Christians willing to join them in these moral causes. This is also what Scripture leads us to expect. Even Abraham, who was the recipient of divine revelation, had to be reproved by the pagan Abimelech for a moral fault (Gen. 20:8-10). The denunciation of pagan societies in the Old Testament makes it clear that they were not without moral sense, and, as we have observed, Romans 2 describes many who had never heard the Old Testament law as having 'the requirements of the law . . . written on their hearts' (v.15). It is this fact of moral awareness amongst unbelievers that makes it possible to persuade whole societies to move nearer to the moral law, at least in their official standards if not in their practice. It is said that when the slave trade was abolished by the British Parliament, there were sixteen evangelical members of Parliament and no more. Yet they won over to their cause an overwhelming majority of the nation and of Parliament, because they had drawn into their moral campaign many people who were not Christians but who could be made to recognize the trade as a horrible evil. It is true even today that there are many non-Christians who are glad of moral leadership and whose consciences are still sensitive on many such issues. Sometimes, like Abimelech, they are even more sensitive than the large number of sleepy or compromised Christians.

Righteousness, justice and peace

How then can we describe the biblical ideals for a fallen world? I suggest that we can best do this in terms of the triple ideals of righteousness, justice and peace. Without righteousness there will be no justice, and without justice there will be little peace. Thus Isaiah 32:15-20 describes the society where 'Justice will dwell in the desert and righteousness live in the fertile field. The fruit of righteousness will be peace; the effect of righteousness will be quietness and confidence for ever. My people will live in peaceful dwelling-places, in secure homes' (vv.16-18). Righteousness must come first and is a far wider term than justice. Those authors who want to make justice the main thing are distorting the biblical picture and end up by neglecting righteousness within marriage, for example.

Now in Israel righteousness was upheld by the law, and in particular by the Ten Commandments. The special status of the Ten Commandments is emphasized in that they alone were written on tables of stone and placed in the ark. For our society today the Ten Commandments still provide an astonishingly complete outline of social righteousness and justice—from care of the old to respect for property and human life and stability in marriage. The Old Testament law, of course, also had a built-in arrangement for the just distribution of the land (the chief form of wealth), with the jubilee and other regulations providing for its redistribution at intervals. Justice at law (only needed because we are fallen) was a major concern, and the punishments fitted the crime. There were no prisons, but frequent arrangements for paying compensation. According to 1 Timothy 1:8-11, the law is there to reprove and restrain sinners. In a fallen world, therefore, we have a practical ideal in terms of the observance of the moral law and the Ten Commandments in particular.

It is sometimes forgotten that in the Bible the law has three uses.[1] *First*, it brings us to conviction of sin and so to Christ (Gal. 3:23-24). *Secondly*, however, it is there to curb, restrain and punish sin, as is shown by the whole network of Old Testament law, and

45

by Romans 13 and 1 Timothy 1:8-11. As a part of this function, it also has a positive role to encourage good (1 Pet. 2:14). In this respect we in Britain have taken too much for granted in the moral values included in many of our laws. Now that many of these things are in danger, we realize how much our lives depended on a Christian tradition of morality. This includes laws about bribery, perjury, Sunday, murder and our relatively just legal system. Even examinations as an alternative to appointment by nepotism, money and social rank have a very substantial Christian origin.

Thirdly, the law provides an outline for the conduct of the believer because it represents God's will and, although the believer is not 'under law' for righteousness, he is still 'under Christ's law' (1 Cor. 9:20-22). If the law represents God's will for society, the Christian cannot brush it on one side. It still outlines His will for the Christian, though our present righteousness must exceed the law's requirements. The Christian, therefore, must live far nearer to the kingdom (or creation) ideal than he can expect society to do. While he himself must do *more* than the law requires (e.g. with respect to divorce), he should aim to get society as close as possible to the law and not expect it to do better.

It is true that real social advances in righteousness, justice and peace have been achieved mainly in periods of history that followed spiritual revivals. But this is not exclusively so, and in any case the benefits of such advances have to be maintained against humanistic and other pressures if we are still to enjoy them. We must also not think only of the broad political arena. The same issues may arise in our own street and in our own small social circle or place of work. It is important to us that our place of work is marked by justice and righteousness, and certainly, if it is not, we are unlikely to have industrial peace. If we are to pray for kings and governors that they will rule in such a way that there is peace, then we are surely to pray for those who control smaller social circles, which may have just as great an impact on our daily lives and give us either relative peace or such conflict and confusion as to make it difficult to live as we are meant to live.

WHAT CAN WE ACHIEVE?

If we care for the good of society as God does, then we shall pray for it (1 Tim. 2:1-2), pay for it (Rom. 13:6) and work for it as God does (Matt. 5:45). We shall be wanting to see an increase in, or at least the maintenance of, such a degree of righteousness, justice and peace as can be achieved in our fallen world.

We have to acknowledge, however, that all such achievements will be only a *matter of degree*, and that we shall often have to settle for the best that we can get in the circumstances, even when it is far below the ideal. (For example, there must be law courts meting out punishments and justice, even though we learn from 1 Corinthians 6 that believers should solve their differences without recourse to such courts.) When the creation ideal cannot be realized, we constantly have to accept the lesser evil or the greater good. This is psychologically difficult for many Christians. They want to stand for the creation ideal—and so they should *for believers*. But if they simply ask for that in Parliament and will not accept less, they are seen as unrealistic Utopians who are too naïve to be listened to. Christians, therefore, find themselves having to support regulations that control gambling, drinking and prostitution so as to limit and restrain them, but also to make them in certain circumstances legal. Yet the Christian believes that gambling and prostitution should be abolished. He knows, however, that to try to do so would only drive them underground, because of the hardness of men's hearts. Sometimes, then, we have to follow the pattern of the Old Testament law and our Lord's commands about divorce and not insist on the creation ideal, even if we are accused by our fellow Christians of compromising.

What are we to say when someone is trying to unscramble the actual chaos into which sin has plunged people? What, for example, do you say is the ideal in the following instances? A couple have been divorced, and both are now remarried to others by whom they have families, and then one of them is converted. How would you seek to help and advise them? Or what do you say to the unconverted couple next door who are living together unmarried? Do you just say, 'Stop!'? Do you tell them to get married, or do you have to work patiently to help them to a more positive view first, if the relationship gives good promise of being stable? The Christian politician is often misunderstood by the church because he seems to be compromising. So is the social worker or even the informal counsellor, if he or she does not always try to push people back to the creation ideal right away. The state of the fallen world means that we cannot undo sin in a hurry, even though we must cling to the biblical ideals and try to get as close as possible to them.

What we can achieve in a fallen world, then, will always be a matter of seeking a greater measure or *degree* of righteousness, justice and peace. We hope to persuade non-Christians of the excellence of Christian standards, firstly by exemplifying them in our own lives, our families and our social and church life and,

47

secondly, by persuading them of the excellence of the law of God. This task is not impossible, as reforms such as the Anti-Slavery and Factory Acts bear witness. Romans 1 and 2 tell us that non-Christians are not devoid of moral sense, and they can often, though not always, see the benefits of righteous living. Christian ethics, we believe, are always best for society, and to some extent we can show this to be the case. Even those who break the moral law usually wish that everyone else would keep it!

Secondly, it needs to be said that improvements on the physical, social and psychological level are *for this life only*, though, as I have tried to argue, that does not mean that we should despise them. The rain and the sun, a healthy body and a brilliant mind do not get anyone nearer to heaven. Indeed, those who enjoy such blessings may make these very things an excuse for claiming that they do not need God. Yet we have to try to be like God in the way we care for people's physical and social welfare, and to live as Jesus did in His concern even to provide food for the hungry. To take another example, marriage guidance counselling should not be regarded as a waste of time. We may be able to help people on a human level, and a background of the law of God in all of its three uses will help us in our thinking on such occasions.

Our practical aim can be described in terms of 'health'—health of body, mind, society and, above all, of spiritual life. The Old Testament word for peace (*shalom*) and the New Testament words for 'sound doctrine' both include this idea of health or health-giving. This is how John prays for Gaius: 'that you may enjoy good health and that all may go well with you, even as your soul is getting along well' (3 John 2). Like the work of a medical doctor, however, the achievement of greater physical health may not in itself lead people to faith at all, though it should cause them to give thanks to God and to seek Him. Such health is good for this life only, but it is nevertheless something for which we must work and pray. The fact that better material and social conditions are for this life only does not lead Paul to despise bodily exercise, but he simply puts it in its true proportion: 'For physical training is of some value, but godliness has value for all things, holding promise for both the present life and the life to come' (1 Tim. 4:8).

Is this worldliness?

There are many godly Christians who fear that a deep concern for the 'this-worldly' needs of people and societies will mean a lessening of concern for personal holiness, the spread of the gospel and a proper Christian view of the transitory nature and inherent evil of 'the world'. When John warns us that we must 'love not the world, neither the things that are in the world' (1 John 2:15 AV), does it not rule out a concern for these more mundane matters? I have written more fully about this elsewhere.[2] Nevertheless, let me say first that we do have to be careful that we are not drawn away from biblical priorities. What, however, are those priorities? Why did Jesus heal people, feed the thousands, turn water into wine, etc.? Why did He insist that the disciples 'come aside and rest awhile'? Was it not because God has given us these bodies and we are intended to look after our own and other people's human (i.e. this-worldly) needs as well as their spiritual needs—even though the latter are more important? The man who therefore neglects his financial obligations to his relatives so as to give all his money to spiritual work is denounced by our Lord (Mark 7:11) and is described by Paul as 'worse than an unbeliever' (1 Tim. 5:8). Certainly, we must not set our love on anything transitory and merely material. We must not allow ourselves to be influenced by the unbiblical priorities of unbelievers. That will always be a battle; but, equally, we must not over-react by taking a negative or ascetic attitude to material things. That would be an example of what Paul describes as 'doctrines of demons' (1 Tim. 4:1 RSV). The devil is apparently as interested in tempting us to despise those good gifts of God which are temporal as in getting us to love them.

It is no criticism of the ministry of godly pastors to say that they, who are rightly preoccupied with things of eternal significance and with the *ministry* of the Word, do not always find it easy to appreciate that there are others who should be preoccupied with the *ministry* (yes, the same Greek word) of tables, as in Acts 6:1-2. The apostles in that chapter kept their distance from meeting the material needs of people themselves, but saw to it that suitably equipped people were set apart by the church for those mundane concerns. In that case it was the physical needs of *believers* that were to be met, but we are to do good to *all* men. Probably it is not the attitude of ministers that causes the trouble here, but a failure of lay people to realize that any ministry other than the ministry of the Word is a Christian ministry at all. If we set preachers on this kind of pedestal, we shall be unbiblical and neglect our duties in other areas.

For this reason I believe that, although there is always a danger in any Christian activity of losing one's way spiritually, there is an equal danger of failing to follow the biblical pattern for fear that we may be overwhelmed. Even close evangelistic contact with unbelievers can be dangerous, but we do not refuse to be so involved for that reason. We simply take suitable precautions, as we must do in any activity.

It is, therefore, only consistent with the rest of the New Testament when Paul, just after his severe warnings about the danger of *loving* money, goes on to tell the rich that God has given us 'richly all things to enjoy' and concludes not that we should shun the good things that riches can buy, but that we should share them (1 Tim. 6:10,17-19). We enjoy living as Christians in God's world and experiencing the blessings of creation, providence and grace. We want others to share them. Of course, it matters to us most of all that they share God's grace, but because we have a positive view of God's creation, we want them also to share the blessings of food, health, family life, education and social peace. The Christian walks a narrow path between covetousness (love of the world, money, etc.) and a pagan asceticism, which is also denounced in no uncertain terms.

The worldliness that the New Testament condemns is found as much in pride, vainglory, the desire to be thought well of by others (including Christians) as in sheer materialism and immorality. We do not escape any of these by trying to avoid contact with those things that we should value as God's gifts but which we must not love or worship.

THE LOCAL CHURCH'S PART

If the individual Christian has a social duty to his neighbour, and may also have a role in social work, counselling or politics, has the local church a part to play? I do not myself believe that the church as such, whether local or national, should be involved in politics, unless there is an absolutely clear-cut moral or religious issue at stake. This requires a fuller discussion. Nevertheless, as I have argued, I do believe that Christian individuals with the necessary gifts not only can but should be involved, looking upon such involvement as a matter of the responsible use of their gifts and as a God-given vocation. If we spend time on the health of our children, why not on the health of our neighbour? The local church, however, does seem to have a particular role in this area which can be described as intermediate.

In his letter to Titus, Paul twice charges him to see that Christians 'apply themselves to good deeds' that are 'profitable to men' (Titus 3:8,14 RSV). It seems no accident that this emphasis on taking seriously people's bodily and other material needs comes most strongly in the pastoral epistles, which were written in late New Testament times when, it seems, there was danger of the church becoming so superspiritual that material needs were

50

neglected. Thus, in 1 Timothy 5:23, Timothy has to be told to take his own physical health seriously. It is in these epistles too that we have the most powerful arguments against asceticism and for a positive enjoyment of the good things of this material life, together with a concern to share them with others (see 1 Tim. 2:1-2; 4:1-10; 5:8,23 and 6:17-19). There is a repeated emphasis on the need to keep the balance: on the one hand, there is a warning of the extreme spiritual danger of the '*love* of money' and, on the other, a positive view of its God-given usefulness. It is possible to be so 'spiritually minded' that we forget that we are to care for whole people.

When the leaders of the early church sought to relieve the physical needs of the saints in Jerusalem, collections were obviously organized on a *church* basis. Individuals were challenged through a letter from Paul, and he hoped that when he came someone would have collected the money so that he could take it as an official gift from 'the churches'. It was not all left to individual philanthropy. Whole congregations were involved. If we are to provide some of the help that is needed today, we too shall have to act informally, and sometimes formally, as a congregation.

Two examples

We can illustrate this first in terms of the problems of unemployment. Each of us can probably do something to help unemployed individuals. Some of us may even be qualified and gifted to do something at local government or national level. Meanwhile, there is a gap between these two levels of involvement, and many local churches have filled it admirably. They have put unemployed Christians in touch with one another, made church buildings available for group activities in the daytime (when no one else is free) and encouraged such a group to meet and share in fellowship, Bible study and activities of a constructive kind for the benefit of others. Such an unemployed group (which is called CHUG—Christian Unemployed Group—in some churches) meets several of the needs of unemployed people that individual help cannot meet.[3] In particular, it puts them in touch with tasks that need doing and that do not take away jobs from others. Such work includes, for example, decorating the homes of old people, gardening, child-minding and shopping for the disabled. A local church can and should think for its locality, while most individuals are either thinking on too small a scale, or on too large a scale, to grapple with problems at that level. There are needs that are simply not met by individual or political action, especially the needs of those who are lonely or have an isolated life-style, such as some retired people and many mothers with young children. Whether its activities are official or unofficial, a local church can encourage its members to be active as a group in tackling problems like those we have just mentioned. Of course, in many churches such activities are one of the great means of evangelistic outreach, even though their immediate aim is to meet people's ordinary needs. While some may feel that these things are best done informally rather than officially in the name of the church, such action will often not take place without the corporate initiative of the local church. Christian Concern for the Mentally Handicapped (formerly A Cause for Concern) is an admirable example of the initiative of a local church leading to the growth of a far wider operation, involving many evangelical churches as well as individuals.

Another practical example might be the problem of dealing with evil influences in schools. What if pornographic literature were circulating in the school that your children attend? You may be able to protect your own children, but presumably we should also be concerned to care for the whole school and the children of other parents, both Christian and non-Christian. We do not wish them to be corrupted. The Parent-Teacher Association (or a similar organization) is a means that is open to us, and an individual Christian could speak up at its meetings; but there is clearly room for groups of Christian parents to take action *together* and speak with one voice against this evil. This is unlikely to be an official church activity, but the church could certainly bring the matter to the attention of parents. It could perhaps co-operate with other evangelical churches to ensure that an effective voice is raised. This may well have an influence which far outweighs the number of Christians involved. Usually there is a good response to any parents who have a positive concern for the needs of a school and have something constructive and useful to say. It may be necessary to ask those in the church who are theologically minded to help their fellow Christians to approach and articulate this problem in such a way that it does not become merely an emotional protest, but rather a well-argued case which others will find hard to answer. It is also true, of course, that there are many parents who are not Christians who may be influenced by such a responsible expression of concern. They may not themselves know how to speak out, but a well-argued case will help them to come out into the open and add their support. This sort of activity has often built very valuable evangelistic bridges with other people, who have some kind of moral concern because they are aware of the moral law, though they may not yet be aware of the gospel.

52

CONCLUSION

Charles Simeon once described his aim in preaching as 'to exalt the Saviour, to humble the sinner and to promote holiness'. Promoting holiness is not merely telling people what they should *not* do; it also involves suggesting positive ways in which holiness must be practised. According to the New Testament this means, above all, practical love for our neighbour. We often cannot provide that practical love except by thinking in terms of the fact that our neighbour is a member of a society which may be responsible for many of his problems; he is not just an isolated individual. The Bible is concerned about the role of the state and other aspects of society, that they may be improved until they minister in a better way to all men.

In the Lord's Prayer we pray that God's will should 'be done on earth, as it is in heaven'. What do we mean when we use those words? It is hard to believe that they can be narrowed to mean only the preaching of the gospel and the life of the believer. The natural meaning would also include a concern for righteousness, justice and peace in the whole community, for good health and for a wide enjoyment of the 'all things' that God has given us 'richly to enjoy'.

If that is so, then our love for all men must extend to the whole of society. Our basic rule for that society will be the moral law, which is to some extent 'written on the hearts' even of many unbelievers, and which is concisely expressed in the Ten Commandments. These enable us to have a policy and to believe that in the goodness of God it may be possible to push society at least a little nearer towards this practical ideal. When we are convinced that it is a part of the will of God, that will be no small thing.

NOTES

1 See Calvin's *Institutes of the Christian Religion,* II, vii, 6-14 (James Clarke, 1962).
2 See O. R. Barclay's *Developing a Christian Mind* (Inter-Varsity Press, 1984), especially chapter 8.
3 See chapter 6 on 'Work and Unemployment'.

QUESTIONS FOR DISCUSSION

a) Should we as a local church be encouraging some of our suitably gifted members to become active in local politics, group actions for the needy or other social action?

b) Should we see the task of a Christian schoolteacher (for instance) as simply that of an evangelist, or how can we support him/her in influencing the moral tone and educational excellence of the school?

c) How can a church, or an individual Christian, avoid being diverted from their evangelistic task if they are involved in social action? What biblical guidelines are there?

FURTHER READING

John R. W. Stott's *Issues Facing Christians Today* (Marshalls, 1984) covers a range of relevant topics. The earlier chapters also deal in fuller detail than this chapter with the biblical basis for social action. The Lausanne Conference Report, *Evangelism and Social Responsibility* (Paternoster, 1982), covers the topic of its title.

A.N. Triton's *Salt to the World: The Christian and Social Involvement* (Inter-Varsity Press, 1978) discusses Christian aims and motives in society, together with some practical implications. *A Christian Social Perspective* by Alan Storkey (Inter-Varsity Press, 1979) provides a solid but well-argued and wide-ranging approach in the Reformed tradition. It owes something to the Amsterdam Christian philosophy and is not light reading. A book which is easy to read, but general, is Abraham Kuyper's *Lectures on Calvinism* (Eerdmans, n.d.). The title is misleading; it is a seminal book on a Christian approach to politics, science, art, etc., by the pioneer of the Dutch Reformed tradition. *Christianity and Civilisation* by Emil Brunner (2 vols, Nisbet, 1947-8) sets out a Lutheran approach; the principles are helpful, but the author was not altogether evangelical. In *Developing a Christian Mind* by Oliver R. Barclay (Inter-Varsity Press, 1984), the chapters on Man, Work and Culture are the most relevant.

The Shaftesbury Project, 79 Maid Marion Way, Nottingham NG1 6AE, is an evangelical organization set up to grapple with Christian thinking about society. Its magazine, *Shaft*, is short but usually pithy. (Since 1986 it has been published in collaboration with the London Institute for Contemporary Christianity and is now called *Christian Impact*.) There are also numerous groups working on different aspects of these questions.

The London Institute for Contemporary Christianity, St Peter's Church, Vere Street, London W1M 9HP, is an organization which has been led by John Stott. It has a considerable variety of longer and shorter courses, evening lectures and weekends, dealing with many aspects of concern under this heading. Joint regional activities are planned under the Shaftesbury Project and London Institute. (Details from the London Institute.)

PART II

The Church in the World

4

The Christian and the State

DONALD MACLEOD

The question of the Christian attitude to politics is a particularly urgent one in the closing decades of the twentieth century. Wherever we turn we face political dilemmas complicated by distinctly religious considerations. In the province of Ulster two Christian traditions engage in violent confrontation. In Southern Africa, apartheid is seen as the only safeguard for the future by one group of Christians and as an affront to human dignity by most others. In South America the struggle for liberation is rooted in an explicit political theology. On a less dramatic level many political issues (for example: abortion, embryo research, nuclear armaments and capital punishment) have distinctly moral and religious overtones. Phenomena such as mass unemployment and urban violence have evoked protest even from sections of the clergy who generally regard politics as none of their business. In the democracies of the West, universal franchise has placed political responsibility firmly on the shoulders of Christians. In the countries of the Soviet bloc, Marxist absolutism has for long meant that the church and politician can live together only in a state of acute tension.

More than ever before, then, Christians have to know the political implications of their faith. This study is a brief attempt to identify the questions and to provide signposts to the answers.

LAYING THE FOUNDATION

The classic biblical statement on the nature of government is given in Romans 13:1-7. Paul insists on three things.

First, *government is a divine appointment:* 'There is no power but by God. The powers that be are ordained by God' (Rom. 13:1). To resist government, therefore, is to resist the ordinance of God (v.2). This has nothing to do with particular forms of government. Paul is not speaking of the divine right of imperialism or the divine right of republicanism, monarchism or democracy. He is speaking of government as such: the *de facto* authority under which Christians find themselves. Its officials are to be respected and honoured, its laws obeyed and its taxes paid 'not only for wrath, but also for conscience sake' (v.5).

Secondly, *government is the servant of God.* This point is made twice in verse 4 using the word *diakonos*. It is also made in verse 6 using the word *leitourgos*. The latter is a more solemn and dignified word but it has no special religious overtones. A *leitourgos* was a public servant.

Paul defines the exact kind of service in three different ways. At one level, it is a service for good, even for *thy* good (v.4). The political system exists not for self-aggrandizement and self-advancement but for the positive good of the community.

At another level, the service performed by the state is that it exercises God's wrath. Private citizens are forbidden to take vengeance for personal wrongs (Rom. 12:19). Vengeance belongs to the Lord. The execution of this vengeance is not left, however, to the day of judgment. Government is the minister of God's vengeance (Rom. 13:4) authorized to express and execute His wrath here and now. It is, literally, to be a terror to evil (Rom. 13:3).

On yet another level, if verse 6 means what it appears to mean, politicians are God's servants for the specific purpose of raising revenue. They impose and collect taxes as God's *leitourgoi*. It is from God that they derive the authority to do so; but it is also to God that they are responsible. Revenues are raised not for their own advantage, nor even in the last analysis for the public good, but for the glory of God.

Thirdly, *government, in its essential nature, is coercive:* it 'bears the sword' (v.4). This may refer to the right to inflict capital punishment, but it cannot be limited to that. It highlights the generally compulsive nature of political authority. It has authority (*exousia*) to enact laws, to impose taxes and to compel compliance with its sanctions.

Paul's immediate concern in this passage is to lay down the basis of obedience to the state. But the principles he sets forth also provide a basis for criticism of the state. Does it respect its own divine appointment? Does it accept its role as servant? Does it use its authority to promote the common good and to deter men of criminal intent? Does it use its revenue in accordance with the will of God? In the last analysis its integrity as government depends on the answers to these questions.

Objectives

Romans 13:1-7 is concerned with general principles. The particular objectives which government ought to pursue are laid down in greater detail in 1 Timothy 2:2, where Paul is directing his readers to pray for those in power. It looks as if what lay behind this was the fact that Christians, experiencing political authority only as a persecuting force, had fallen into a kind of inverted spiritual snobbery. Politicians (and the upper classes in general) could not be saved and therefore should not be prayed for. Paul goes to the theological heart of the problem in saying that God 'will have all men [including politicians] to be saved' (v.4). On this basis he directs that prayer is to be made for all who are in authority. He also lays it down that such prayer is to refer specifically to their political responsibilities: 'that we may lead quiet and peaceful lives in all godliness and honour' (v.2). Implicit in that prayer are four political objectives.

First, *the maintenance of internal peace and security*. This involves the provision of effective policing. But it also involves constant care to minimize the discontent which breeds friction and discord. Politicians, like parents, must avoid provoking the resentment of those under their authority (Eph. 6:4).

Secondly, *politicians must promote international peace*. War is the greatest of all political evils and every legitimate step must be taken to prevent it. One such step is the maintenance of a defence force strong enough to deter any potential aggressor. However, peace cannot be secured by military methods alone. States must cultivate good relations with their neighbours through constant interaction at diplomatic, cultural, sporting and commercial levels. They must practise forbearance in the face of insult and injury. They must forge peace treaties and alliances. Above all, they should (with the church's enthusiastic assistance) actively discourage all national arrogance and jingoism.

Thirdly, *politicians are to pursue policies which will make it possible for their people to live with honour*. Men are made in the image of God and their environment should be commensurate with that. Human beings should not be degraded by squalor, destitution, oppression, ugliness and unemployment. They should be able to earn their bread, albeit by the sweat of their brows. They should be free. They should be able to express their creativity. They should be cared for in illness and old age. They should be educated. Their general surroundings should not jar on their God-given aesthetic sensitivities. (It is surely significant, not least for local authorities, that the very first thing we are told about the

61

environment in which God placed man is that it contained 'every tree that is pleasant to the sight'—Gen. 2:9). Today it is virtually impossible to live with honour in the shanty towns of the Third World or the concrete jungles of Western cities.

Fourthly, *government has a responsibility in connection with godliness*, at least to the extent that, *as God's servant*, it is bound to provide a framework within which godliness can flourish. This means, for example, guaranteeing religious freedom, something which has never come easily to politicians. Such freedom must include not merely the guaranteed right to practise one's own religion, but also the right to evangelize and proselytize (the Soviet bloc countries in general grant the former but deny the latter). The state should also ensure that converts do not suffer civil and social disabilities when they change from one religion to another.

Again, government promotes godliness by its example. To some extent this is a matter of the life-style of the individuals in power. Whether they live for God or against, the prestige of their office enhances their influence. But there is also the influence of official, collective government attitudes. If meetings are preceded by prayer, if acknowledgment is made of accountability to God, if respect is shown to His Word, if policy is informed by Christian principle and compassion, the government is making a positive contribution towards the formation of a general Christian ethos.

More important still, government promotes godliness by legislating in accordance with divine standards. The logical (or theological) basis for this lies in the fact that the political process is God's servant. As such, it has no right either to make its own rules or to ignore God's rules. In the abstract it has no right, either, to impose only sociological law, that is, law which is socially useful and acceptable. If the legislative process is not rooted in juridical norms which are themselves rooted in the nature of God, we face chaos. Most Christians seem to feel instinctively that the inevitable result of legislative relativism would be greater laxity. But this is naïve. The result will be lawlessness, and that, given the depravity of man, is more likely to lead to harshness than to laxity. In fact, the increasing number of exemplary and deterrent (as opposed to equitable) sentences being imposed by judges and magistrates already fills one with foreboding. Once we abandon God's norms, we have nothing but man's whim.

It is at this point that we run into a serious problem. We live in a pluralistic society composed of people of many faiths and people of no faith at all. This inevitably sets limits to the imposition of Christian standards. As Christians we cannot persecute. We have no right to use the compulsive power of the state to impose conformity with our own religion or to prevent other people practising theirs. We must grant to others the same religious freedom as we claim for ourselves. What then is left to us so far as imposing Christian standards is concerned?

It remains, surely, that we can still expect government to enact laws which conform to 'the light of nature'. The Gentiles, says Paul, show by their actions that the law of God is written on their hearts and that they have consciences which constantly praise or blame them in terms of that law (Rom. 2:14-15). Added political force is given to this by the fact that the authority of the Decalogue is recognized not only by Christians but also by Jews and Muslims. It seems not only right but practical, therefore, to argue that government legislation should conform to the Ten Commandments.

Practical Implications

But what does this mean in practice?

First, *recognition of the sanctity of life*. There must be adequate penal sanctions against homicide in all its forms and against all kinds of violence against the person. These must apply in all their force to abortion and euthanasia as well as to the whole field of embryo research. The protective fences must be set up not around some secondary characteristic of humanness (consciousness, dependence, creativity, quality of life) but around humanness itself. The comatose, the unborn and the handicapped, precisely because of their weakness, need the full protection of the law.

Secondly, *the sanctity of truth*. Perjury strikes at the heart of our whole legal system, and commercial life becomes impossible if contracts are lightly broken. At this point one also has to worry about the knock-on effect of dishonesty in the political process itself (for example, the breaking of electoral pledges and reneging on international agreements). The words of John MacMurray deserve to be pondered: 'You can't expect people to retain their confidence in money when they have lost their confidence in men'.[1]

Thirdly, *the sanctity of property*. Because property-owners have such power (one might even say disproportionate power) in Western society today, this is the best protected of all the sanctities. Indeed, existing law in this connection probably requires to be counterbalanced by some of the humanitarian principles of the Bible, such as, for example, the one laid down in Exodus 22:26-27: 'If ever you take your neighbour's garment in pledge, you shall restore it to him before the sun goes down; for that is his only covering, it is his mantle for his body; in what else should he sleep?

63

and if he cries to me, I will hear, for I am compassionate.' Should the principle of the limited liability of creditors not be extended to all men, and not only to worldly-wise commercial companies?

It is reasonable to expect, too, that legislation on *marriage* will reflect biblical norms. This will be evident in such details, for example, as the banning of bigamy and polygamy, and the recognition of the principle that there are prohibited degrees of consanguinity. The indissolubility of marriage would also be recognized in so far as provision for divorce would be carefully controlled. This would mean ideally that divorce would be possible only on strictly biblical grounds (adultery, and irremediable desertion?). In practice, however, and especially in a pluralistic society, Christians would have to ponder whether account should not be taken of the principle which lay behind the Mosaic divorce laws, namely, the hardness of men's hearts (Matt. 19:8). It may be necessary to distinguish between what is tolerable for church members and what can be expected of the community in general.

Finally, *legal recognition should be given to the sanctity of a man's reputation.* This must include protection against defamation. But the time has come to consider also whether there should not be legal protection against press harassment. Individuals have the right, of course, to refuse to talk to the press; but things have now come to such a pass that the statement, 'Mr. MacLeod refused to talk to us', itself has sinister overtones. Such a man, it is implied, clearly has something to hide.

Problematic Areas

Legislation in all these areas would be fairly practicable because it would command the respect of most members of the community. But there are other areas where legislation would be more problematical.

One of these is the question of Sunday. Today the idea of the Puritan Sabbath is unacceptable to all but a tiny minority even of the Christian community itself. That does not affect the principle itself or even the duty of the state to legislate according to God's will, but it does affect the practicability of such legislation. No doubt, government could enforce it even against the active opposition of most of the population, but such enforcement would be seen by men as persecution. What we do have a right to expect, however, is that government will recognize the humanitarian aspects of the Sabbath. There must be protection against the economic pressures which demand a seven-day working week. The issue also involves a basic question of religious freedom. A

Christian is not free to practise his religion if he is forced to work on its holy days.

Another problematical area is the Decalogue's prohibition of idolatry. The proper application of this, now that the theocracy is a thing of the past, is within the church itself. Church members guilty of idolatry should be subjected to the church's own discipline. But to extend the law to the wider community would be dangerous. Hinduism, Buddhism and possibly Islam are idolatrous religions. To ban idolatry would be to ban these religions, and this would be a betrayal of religious freedom. Christians committed to toleration are bound to grant other religions the same freedom as they claim for themselves.

We run into similar difficulties in connection with blasphemy. It is very difficult to draft a workable parliamentary statute on this issue, because in a pluralistic society the law would have to protect objects of religious veneration in general. The net result would be the prohibition of all that would 'wound and outrage' the feelings of devotees of religions of all kinds. This might indeed prevent the televising of films which blaspheme the name of Jesus Christ. But it would also, almost inevitably, make it impossible to engage in legitimate criticism of the papacy, Islam and the Moonies. Besides, so far as protecting the Christian faith is concerned, it is very doubtful whether the state is competent to define blasphemy. We should be expecting of judges a degree of theological competence they do not possess: or, alternatively, exposing ourselves to the subjective judgments of juries as to what is scurrilous, indecent or contemptuous.

Education is a special problem. On the face of things it should be possible to provide a purely secular education, making no provision at all for religious education. When we probe a little deeper, however, difficulties quickly appear. Because religion cannot be insulated from other areas of life, it will inevitably crop up throughout the curriculum. It will affect the teaching of history and the critical study of literature. Even more directly, it will affect the various departments of science. The teaching of evolution and the banning of creationism, for example, reflect a religious judgment. When we move into such sensitive areas as sex education the difficulties are even more acute. Indeed the very decision to teach it may reflect a deliberate attack on the Christian idea of modesty. The plea that the subject is taught without moral judgments is no defence. It merely reflects a religious or metaphysical judgment that sexuality and morality are in principle separable.

But the real problem lies deeper still. So-called secular education is an attempt to divorce education from metaphysics. Teachers are to operate with no agreed view on the origin of the universe, and with no agreed value-system. But this makes it impossible to answer (or even to ask) the most basic questions about education. What is its meaning? What are its goals? What are to be its methods? What is to be the content of our science lessons, bearing in mind, for example, that modern physics quickly brings us face to face with metaphysics? What criteria are we to apply in making literary and historical judgments?

It seems inescapable that state education must identify itself, for the sake of coherence, with one particular world-view. It also seems inescapable that in Britain that should be not Marxism or Humanism or Islam, but Christianity. The final reason for that, of course, is that it is true. But there are others of a more political complexion: it is the religion which commands the most adherents; it has shaped our culture; it has moulded our institutions; it has permeated our history; it is enshrined in our constitution (the Thirty-Nine Articles, the Westminster Confession and the Corona-tion Oath to maintain the Protestant religion are integral parts of our legal system).

Kenosis

But if the question is one of imposing Christian standards, there is something deeper than anything we have mentioned so far. Do we impose the Christian emphasis on *kenosis*: self-emptying, making oneself nothing? Do we try to imbue our national diplomacy and our whole internal political machinery with the spirit of Matthew 5:39, 'Whosoever shall smite thee on thy right cheek, turn to him the other also'?

The instinctive evangelical response to such questions would be that these principles can apply only to private conduct; if applied to public life and to the state they would be disastrous. We should not automatically endorse this instinct; we should examine it. *Kenosis* means acting without regard to one's own interest. This has certainly been a very rare phenomenon in political history: 'Nations are not to be trusted beyond their own interest', said George Washington. But are we prepared to elevate this to the status of a moral principle, and even to endorse Reinhold Niebuhr's famous (and dreadful) thesis that although man the individual is moral, man in society is immoral? Niebuhr speaks of 'the brutal character of the behaviour of all human collectives, and the power of self-interest and collective egoism in all inter-group relations'. Consequently, the pronouncements of moralists, sociologists and educators lead to confusion, because 'they fail to recognise those elements in man's collective behaviour which belong to the order of nature and can never be brought completely under the dominion of reason and conscience'. Not surprisingly, Niebuhr is sceptical of the expectations of Christian idealists: 'The demand of religious moralists that nations subject themselves "to the law of Christ" is an unrealistic demand, and the hope that they will do so is a sentimental one.'[2]

The picture drawn in these statements is only too true as a matter of history. Yet it cannot be true as an affirmation of the way God requires us to live. The church itself, for example, is a community, but it cannot shake itself free of the implications of the claim that it is 'the only society on earth which exists for the benefit of non-members'. Besides, communities, no less than individuals, are bound by the divine imperative of love. They are bound to look not at their own things but at the things of others, and to be obsessed not with their rights but with their obligations. The state's (necessary) resisting of evil is no breach of this principle, because it is then executing not its own wrath but God's.

It seems clear that no state or group has the right to vindicate its own honour or to pursue its own advantage regardless of the needs of others. The Protestants of Ulster must practise *kenosis* in relation to their Catholic fellow-citizens. The rich nations of the North must practise *kenosis* in relation to the poor countries of the South. And a community asked to accept a military establishment on its doorstep must practise *kenosis*, even though that means becoming a prime target in the event of nuclear war.

THE CHURCH AND POLITICS

One hears often, from both politicians and churchmen, that the church should not be involved in politics. The plea is not merely that it should not be involved in party politics (which few would deny), but that it should not express political judgments either collectively or through its official spokesmen.

This plea can be backed with plausible arguments. For example, Jesus took no part in politics. Neither did the early church. But such arguments carry little weight. There is a radical contrast between our position today and that of the early church. The latter possessed no political power and therefore never faced the question of what to do with it. We, by contrast, do possess it both by virtue of our personal franchise and by virtue of our collective influence. The media and the political authorities may even approach the church to ask what it thinks. This happened, for example, in connection with the Warnock Report, to which many Christian bodies were asked to make submissions. Our political power is a reality and we must have some coherent philosophy as to how to use it.

Besides, it really is not true that Jesus made no political pronouncements. When He said, 'Render . . . to Caesar the things that are Caesar's' (Matt. 22:21), He was expressing an opinion on a very sensitive political issue of the time, namely, Was it lawful to pay the imperial taxes or not? When He called Herod 'that fox' (Luke 13:32), He was making a political comment. When He included a Zealot and a tax-gatherer among the disciples, He was making political comment. When He spoke of the leaders of His day devouring widows' houses, He was making political comment (Matt. 23:14). Obviously, Jesus did not take the line adopted by many preachers today that you should stay above politics because otherwise you lose your credibility and thus the power to do men good. He managed instead to offend all the political groupings of His day: the Pharisees, the Sadducees, the Zealots and, at last, the Romans.

In any case, we have no right to build theological conclusions on the slender foundation of the alleged silences of Jesus and the early church. Our canon is the entire Scripture, including the Old Testament, and when we consult it we find abundant support for involvement in politics on the part of Christian leaders. Many of the outstanding figures of the Old Testament (Abraham, Joseph, Moses, Samuel, David, Solomon) participated actively in the political process. Great prophets like Elijah and Elisha, Isaiah and Jeremiah, Amos and Hosea, made overtly political comments. Nor was this true only in the context of the theocracy. A post-exilic figure like Daniel also found his vocation in politics and went to the very top, despite the enormous gulf between the culture in which he worked and his own personal beliefs. At the same time, he was one of the chosen instruments of God's self-disclosure: a clear embodiment of the legitimacy of combining in one man the role of prophet and politician.

It is not only that the arguments *against* the church's involvement in politics are untenable, however. There are also good positive reasons *for* such involvement.

Firstly, *the church must guide its people in their use of the franchise*. This cannot mean, of course, giving detailed directions as to the party to vote for. But some attempt must be made to develop a Christian political consciousness. Church members should at least be able to apply biblical criteria to the claims of the candidates and to the programmes proposed by the various parties.

Secondly, *there is a need to give guidance to individual Christians who are actively involved in politics.* After all, the church does this for Christian husbands and wives, parents and children, masters and servants (provided it expounds the whole counsel of God, including Ephesians 5:22—6:9). The very fact that the politicians' world is so stressful and so spiritually dangerous makes the church's ministry in this connection all the more vital.

Thirdly, *the church, through its official teachers, has to expound the political principles laid down in the Bible.* A preacher has no right, for example, deliberately to ignore Deuteronomy 17:14 ff. or Romans 13:1-7; nor can he discharge his responsibility by a superficial, detached exegesis of these passages. He has to *preach* them, relating the principles they contain to the world in which he and his hearers live. After all, it is application that makes a sermon.

There are times, too, when the church must express God's judgment on politicians and on the political process. Samuel did so in the case of Saul: 'Because thou hast rejected the word of the Lord, he hath also rejected thee from being king' (1 Sam. 15:23). Nathan, Elijah, Elisha and Jeremiah, in their differing situations, did the same. It is entirely appropriate that government policies be weighed in the moral balances of the church and, if found wanting, faithfully condemned.

Conversely, the church should also *encourage* government. This is especially important at times when its policies are right but unpopular. It is worth considering whether there is not an imbalance in the church's ministry in this whole area. Our instinct is to speak out when we disapprove. We ought perhaps to give more attention to a ministry of consolation.

It is often said that the church should leave political comment and political involvement to individual Christians and keep itself officially aloof and unsullied. Part of the answer to that must be that the church, as a group, has its own moral responsibilities. It must express its love and concern collectively, in relation to its own members, to other groups and to the state. It is precisely in the context of the worship of the assembled community that Paul lays it down that prayer and supplication must be made for kings and for all in authority (1 Tim. 2:1-2). Furthermore, how often does the individual feel so utterly helpless! He has no power! no influence! What is his voice amid the babel of confusing noises? By comparison, the church has organization, visibility, influence and power. It must use these responsibly and caringly, bearing in mind that it was precisely to the church as a community that the Lord said, 'You are the salt of the earth . . . You are the light of the world' (Matt. 5:13,14). It serves society both by the example

69

of its own internal life and by its dynamic and *kenotic* concern for groups other than itself; and even for groups in competition with itself.

Guiding principles

Suppose the church, then, commits itself to being involved. What principles should guide it?

First, it should commit itself to *Christian methods of argument*. We live in an age of pressure-groups committed to the use of non-rational means of persuasion: marches, demonstrations, sit-ins, picketings, slogans, industrial action. The church is the community of the Word, of *logos*, of reason. It is also committed to regarding man as made in the image of God, and forbidden to use carnal weapons (2 Cor. 10:4). It has no right to resort to violence. Even the violence of so-called passive resistance is ruled out except in the gravest circumstances. Neither has it any right, in its evangelism or in its wider prophetic ministry, to use means of persuasion inconsistent with the spirit of the gospel or its basic respect for human dignity.

On the other hand, in its attempts to persuade, the church must use arguments which have *political validity*. It often finds it difficult to do so, because such arguments can look very unspiritual and even very like a betrayal of the gospel. The temptation to appeal to the absolute authority of God and the infallibility of Scripture is strong. Sunday trading contravenes the fourth commandment, and that's that. Abortion contravenes the sixth. It also goes against the description of embryonic life given in Psalm 139 and in the story of John the Baptist. Such arguments are indeed faithful and even touching. But are they wise? Do they reflect Daniel's approach to the chief of the eunuchs in Daniel 1:8 ff. or Paul's approach to the Athenians in Acts 17:22 ff.? What we have to ask ourselves is whether we are really trying to communicate with the powers that be, or merely salving our own consciences and making reassuring noises to our own community. If we are genuinely trying to communicate and genuinely trying to affect the political process, then we must speak *ad hominem*. We must speak to government where it is; and where it is at the moment, it cannot understand (or even hear) arguments based on the Bible and theology. It can only understand arguments addressed to conscience and to prudence: arguments which show the human-itarian, social and economic advantages of Christian proposals. We know, as believers, that something is right because it is biblical. We may even feel it right to tell them that that is our starting-point. But

70

in the last analysis we must put before them the political advantages of what we plead for.

Again, the church must pursue *social justice*, not merely law and order. Here again is something which it is easy to overlook. There is so much that we want to outlaw and condemn. The church is pro-police, pro-hanging, pro stiffer jail sentences, pro-discipline; and anti-abortion, anti-union, anti-strikes and anti-terrorism. All that, in normal circumstances, is right and proper. But we dare not overlook the fact that there may be law and order where there is no justice, and indeed that sometimes the forces of law and order are themselves precisely the forces of injustice. There is law and order in a labour-camp, but there is no justice. There was law and order in the Scottish Highlands during the Clearances,[3] but there was no justice. In Britain today, there is still structural injustice. Economic and industrial power is concentrated in the hands of a tiny minority able to command financial rewards out of all proportion to their actual work. The majority, whether in management or on the shop-floor, work for wages which, by comparison, are trivial; and at any time they may find themselves redundant as a result of decisions taken in board-rooms which have little understanding of ordinary human problems. Fortunes are inherited, not made. Add the problems of long-term unemployment, of poor housing, of regional inequality, of racial discrimination, and it is not surprising that there are occasional outbursts of lawlessness. It is not good enough for the church merely to condemn these. It must look at the injustices against which the violence is a protest, however irrational and sometimes even destructive the outbursts may be. It must not stand with privilege against the deprived, with wealth against poverty, with power against weakness. It must not merely call for riots to be quelled, terrorists to be shot, and order to be imposed. It must call for justice: for the society of its dreams, in which righteousness prevails, in which opportunity does not depend on accidents of birth and residence, and in which men and women of all races, creeds and classes have equal access to jobs, to schools and hospitals and to the mountains and the rivers.[4]

This means that the church must see things from below, not from above. This again is something it finds very difficult. The churches, especially Reformed churches, are often composed of the fit and the strong, the intelligent and the healthy. They have been hard-working and successful. Very often, the membership has little experience of unemployment or social discrimination or poor housing or inner-city deprivation or rural hardship. It is very difficult for such people to see things from below. 'How', wrote Solzhenitsyn, 'can you expect a man who's warm to understand one who's cold?'[5] We see from the top, through the eyes of privilege and strength and success. We even tend to give these things a moral rating. Our success is the reward for our own labour. Other people's failure (and poverty) reflects only their moral weakness.

However difficult the exercise may be, we must try, as the church of God, to reverse this whole perspective. Christ, having become flesh, dwelt among the poor and deliberately identified with the broken-hearted, the captives, the blind and the bruised (Luke 4:18). This was how His mission was seen even from the standpoint of the Old Testament: 'He shall vindicate the poor of the people, he shall save the children of the needy, and shall break in pieces the oppressor' (Ps. 72:4). We, with Him, look at the world from the cross, viewing it through the eyes of the weak and powerless, the dumb and speechless, the despised and rejected. The church cannot even stand even-handedly between the rich and the poor, as if they were equally right, and equally wrong, and engaged in a battle in which each has a fair chance. There is a profound asymmetry between the forces of poverty and the forces of privilege. A multinational company and its employees are not evenly balanced. Striking teachers and their pupils are not evenly balanced. Blacks and whites in South Africa are not evenly balanced. The church must note this asymmetry and speak accordingly: speaking more often for the poor than for the rich, speaking more loudly, speaking in the accents of overstatement, because even then it can scarcely gain a hearing above the propaganda generated by the forces of privilege. Political power, economic power and media power are in the hands of those who benefit from current injustices. That is why privilege argues against social change; and why the pursuit of justice always labours under the disadvantage of appearing subversive. 'No society has ever achieved peace without incorporating injustice into its harmony', wrote Reinhold Niebuhr; 'Those who would eliminate the injustice are therefore always placed at the moral disadvantage of imperilling its peace.'[6] If the church is going to identify with the poor, it will inevitably speak asymmetrically and thus leave itself open to the charge of being unbalanced and subversive.

This makes it all the more important that when the church does speak out it should confine itself to issues on which it can speak *a genuine word from the Lord*. Its political sagacity is no greater than that of any other institution and may even be less. Its ministry is valid only as it remains a ministry of the Word, speaking forth the ethical and theological judgments of Scripture.

Does this mean that the church must confine itself to general principles and never venture to give detailed advice? Is its duty done when it proclaims the need for a 'just, caring and participatory' society, or something equally nebulous, and should it then hold its peace?

By no means. Many of the most acute political problems facing us today have significant moral and theological components on which the church has every right to comment. Mass unemployment, for example, is an assault on human dignity, making it impossible for men to live honourably, placing an often intolerable strain on family life, and provoking resentments which inevitably erupt in violence and disorder. The problems of Ulster have an obvious religious weighting. So does apartheid. So, too, do the questions of overseas aid, nuclear defence and conditions in our prisons. These are all issues on which the church has a right to express its concern. At the local level, too, there will inevitably be issues which pose a moral threat to the community: for example, over-supply of liquor licences, police tactics, decisions of local education authorities, plans to build defence installations, inadequate medical facilities, and proposals to shut down production units run by nationalized industries. The church's voice on such issues will not run on consistent party lines; nor will it always be speaking *for* the community. It may sometimes be disturbed by the local consensus and should say so. What it cannot do is to stand aloof from such discussions.

There are other issues which are directly and specifically moral, on which the church is more expert than government and on which its views ought to be not only welcomed but solicited and, when received, treated with respect. The most obvious of these are abortion, euthanasia, embryo research and divorce. The tragedy, of course, is that the church does not speak with anything like a unanimous voice. Because it has abandoned the normative criterion of Scripture, its pronouncements are as shallow and as varied as the personal prejudices of its clergy. It is the lack of authority, rather than the lack of opportunity, that has destroyed the credibility of the church.

It may be said in reply to all this that it amounts to letting the world set the agenda. One has some sympathy with this. The church's primary role is a preaching one, and if in its preaching it observes biblical proportion and balance, its political profile will be fairly low. There is a sense, however, in which the world does set the agenda: not by the preoccupations of its politicians and journalists but by its own need. Take the Good Samaritan, for example. For him the agenda was set by the needs of the poor fellow who was attacked and robbed. By contrast, the priest and the Levite are classic examples of refusing to let the world set the agenda. The messages of the great prophets took their contours not only from the religious but also from the social problems of their day. And even for Christ Himself, the agenda was set by the world into which He came. He did not claim to be so busy preaching that He had no time to attend to the sick, the paralytic and the demon-possessed. The church is Christ's representative in society. It must function as salt and light in every sphere of human activity. It must reflect its Lord's attitude to the whole range of human need. The most important area of need may indeed be spiritual. But men are weary and heavy-laden with other burdens too, crushed into the ground by oppression, hunger and poverty. The moment we begin to sympathize with them, we are moving into political involvement, however minimal, and to that extent letting the world set the agenda.

NOTES

1 J. MacMurray, *Freedom in the Modern World* (Faber, 1968), p.43.
2 R. Niebuhr, *Moral Man and Immoral Society* (Scribner, 1960), pp.xx,xii,75.
3 Between 1815 and 1886 many landowners in the Scottish Highlands drove the people off the land to make way for sheep. This led to appalling hardship, relieved only by mass emigration.
4 There is an admitted tension between using political arguments, as advocated a little earlier in the chapter, and calling for the society of our dreams. I am not sure, however, that it is wise to try to eliminate such tensions. If pressed, I would probably say that the use of politically valid arguments is one way towards achieving the society of our dreams. The tension is mitigated by the fact that the one refers to means, the other to ends.
5 Solzhenitsyn, *A Day in the Life of Ivan Denisovich* (Penguin, 1963), p.23.
6 R. Niebuhr, p.129.

QUESTIONS FOR DISCUSSION

a) 'Paul's immediate concern in Romans 13:1-7 is to lay down the basis of obedience to the state. But the principles he sets forth also provide a basis for criticism of the state' (p.60). Drawing on the principles mentioned at the beginning of this chapter, how would you assess the central policies of the major political parties? Are there any grounds on which an argument for the future creation of a Christian political party might be advanced?

b) How is the Christian to demonstrate the case for the incorporation of biblical standards governing Sundays, idolatry, blasphemy or education into legislation in our society?

c) How should the principle of 'seeing things from below' be worked out in the witness of our own local church?

FURTHER READING

The best material is to be found in the standard commentaries on the relevant biblical passages. The following list includes works cited in the text plus some recommendations for further reading:

J. Calvin, *Institutes of the Christian Religion*, IV, xx (James Clarke, 1962)

H. F. R. Catherwood, *The Christian Citizen* (Hodder & Stoughton, 1969)

H. F. R. Catherwood, *A Better Way: The Case for a Christian Social Order* (Inter-Varsity Press, 1975)

J. K. Galbraith, *The Anatomy of Power* (Corgi Books, 1983)

J. MacMurray, *Freedom in the Modern World* (Faber, 1968)

R. Niebuhr, *Moral Man and Immoral Society* (New York, Scribner, 1960; Edinburgh, T. & T. Clark (distrib.), 1960)

S. Rutherford, *Lex Rex; or, The Law and the Prince* (c. 1644). Available in *The Presbyterian's Armoury* (Robert Ogle and Oliver & Boyd, 1843), vol.3

F. A. Schaeffer, *A Christian Manifesto* (Pickering & Inglis, 1982)

J. A. Walter, *Fair Shares* (The Handsel Press, 1985)

The Christian and the State in Revolutionary Times (Westminster Conference). This volume contains the papers read at the 1975 Conference.

D. F. Wright, *Essays in Evangelical Social Ethics* (Paternoster, n.d.). The essay by Haddon Wilmer, 'Towards a Theology of the State', virtually dismisses the New Testament teaching as irrelevant to the present day.

5

The Inner City

PAUL BASSETT

In post-war Britain the inner city has re-emerged as a focus of
social concern. One of the contributory factors has been the large
movement of the population away from our city centres, their
living accommodation often being replaced by high-rise office
blocks. Large areas were destroyed by the heavy bombing raids of
World War II. Where the city dwellers remained, they were often
rehoused, particularly in the fifties and sixties, in a concrete jungle
environment of skyscraper blocks of flats. But the pioneers' dream
often became a social and moral nightmare. The terraced houses of
the Victorian era, though drab, cramped and deficient in certain
domestic facilities, had created and sustained a closely knit community where neighbourliness and care were paramount. The brave
new world development, however, led to many new social problems. Tenants now suffered from a sense of isolation and became
self-imprisoned in their own homes. Crime continued to escalate
throughout our land, but more especially in the cities. Indeed in
some of our cities nowadays it is a brave person who will venture
out after nightfall; there is always the fear of attack by a rapist or
mugger. From the mid-1960s successive governments began to
adopt policies directed towards these problems. Key issues of concern were these: to alleviate disadvantages, improve the environment and housing conditions, and develop community life with
adequate recreational facilities.

Yet, having painted that general picture, we must add that no
two cities are alike. In some, the commuters leave at night for
suburbia or the land of the Green Belt. In others, a large proportion of the population still live in the inner-city environment, in terraced houses, blocks of flats, hostels or bedsitters. Here there is
plenty of night life, as discos, casinos, night clubs and cinemas
abound.

What has been said above applies in large measure also to the new housing estates. Like the inner-city areas, these have always presented the church with a great challenge, and also with certain underlying problems. Sometimes these people too feel isolated geographically and cut off from others in their towns and cities. In some cases they are the overspill from relatively distant areas and have therefore lost their identity. Occasionally, former criminals and problem families have been housed in these estates, and so they have come to be regarded as undesirable and even notorious places in which to live.

THE NEED FOR EVANGELISM

How is the church to evangelize such needy areas as inner cities or housing estates? we may ask. It must be recognized that while the inner city is a new sociological phenomenon it is not new spiritually. God has always called the church to city evangelism. We must begin in *our* Jerusalem; we must stand where the apostle Paul stood and believe that Christ will give us a similar vision of the lost. Every city worker needs to open his Bible and read: 'Then spake the Lord to Paul in the night by a vision, Be not afraid, but speak, and hold not thy peace: for I am with thee, and no man shall set on thee to hurt thee: for I have much people in this city' (Acts 18:9-10). The trouble is that instead of making a fearless proclamation of the gospel, we can so easily be paralysed into fearful silence by the seeming hopelessness of the task confronting us. But we *must* speak: not only does God command us to do so, but He promises us His presence and, most of all, assures us that He has 'much people' there. We need to remember that God's people have been confronted before by 'cities walled, and very great', and that they too saw themselves as 'grasshoppers' beside the city-dwellers who were 'men of a great stature' (Num. 13:28,32,33). But God can still raise up His giant-killers with their spiritual slings and five smooth stones. He still has His 'Calebs' for inner-city leadership — men who can 'still the people' and say, 'Let us go up at once, and possess it; for we are well able to overcome it' (v.30).

Yes, there are British cities 'straitly shut up', as Jericho was. We then must become like Joshua, who 'lifted up his eyes, and looked, and, behold, there stood a man over against him with his sword drawn in his hand' (Josh. 5:13). Christ will most certainly come to our rescue, as He came to Joshua's at Jericho. Here must be our starting-point. We stand in our city centres on sinful ground; yet, with Christ the Captain of the Lord's host beside us, we too are

78

told: 'Loose thy shoe from off thy foot, for the place whereon thou standest is holy' (v.15). Only then do we dare to rise to our feet and by faith 'compass the city' (6:3), until the walls of opposition and indifference fall before the drawn two-edged sword of God's Word. Let us blow upon our gospel trumpets and 'Shout; for the Lord hath given you the city' (6:16).

We need to remember that men of God have stood where we now stand and, with God-given courage and indomitable spirit, have tackled the seemingly impossible task of winning wicked cities for God. The words of Dr Campbell Morgan are worth recalling. When God brought him to Westminster Chapel in London, where the situation facing him seemed too far gone to be changed, he said to his people: 'I come with a passionate conviction that the church is renegade when she abandons great centres to the devil.'

Perhaps we are dogged by another temptation, namely, that we are not personally equipped to undertake the difficult task of inner-city evangelism. The scholarly saint, Thomas Chalmers, might well have thought the same a century ago, but that was far from being the case. He was one of the most advanced social reformers that Scotland ever produced, writing much on economics generally, and in particular on charity and the Poor Law as it operated in his day. Scarcely had he finished his significant contribution in bringing to birth the Free Church of Scotland when Chalmers began to look around for the worst district to be found in the city of Edinburgh, intending to make this the object of his care. It was on the West Port that he fixed his choice, an infamous area which had been the scene of several cold-blooded murders. Of its 2,000 people, 1,500 had had no contact at all with the church. They lived in filthy closes, abounding in drunkenness and all kinds of vice. These perishing souls immediately caught his vision and captured his heart. Casting aside his convenerships and all other church work (apart from his professorship), he gave himself to the West Port Mission. Gathering round him some like-minded Christians, he divided the area into districts and appointed a visitor to each, encouraging them to get to know the people and to read God's Word to them.

Progress was slow, but the zeal of Chalmers drove them all relentlessly on. After a year, a loft was acquired for meetings; but the greatest misgivings were felt when, despite all those months of evangelism, the first meeting was attended by only twelve adults, mostly old women. Prayer was increased, and in the end the fruit came. Through the prayers and persistent outreach of Chalmers and his team of visitors, a building was erected in which 520 people gathered for worship. One old man, dying without faith, was asked if he wanted a minister to visit him. 'Yes,' he said, 'I want that zealous man Chalmers, whom I turned from my door 39 times.'[1]

THE CHALLENGE OF THE INNER CITIES

The above brief survey of former ventures in city evangelism is necessary if we are to appreciate that the work to which we are called is hard and unglamorous. It is in our inner cities that we generally find the red-light areas, where crime and prostitution abound. The inner-city dwellers are mainly poor, whereas the challenge comes to a church that is chiefly middle-class. Never was there a time when we needed more to remember that 'God is no respecter of persons' and that 'the common people heard him gladly' (Acts 10:34; Mark 12:37).

How shall we begin? Firstly, by realizing that God has called us to 'preach the gospel to every creature' (Mark 16:15). We must continue to do this faithfully in our churches, and to encourage our people to bring in the unsaved. What has happened in some congregations is that, because unbelievers are not coming in at night, a further 'meal' has been given to the Christians in place of preaching the gospel. This is, humanly speaking, quite logical. Why preach the gospel to the converted? Yet such a minister and people not only lose their vision for the lost, but tend to become almost totally inward-looking, blind to and removed from the needs of the city around them. We are not unaware, of course, that in our cities fear is often a contributory factor, keeping unbelievers and sometimes believers from attending services, especially at night. But it does need to be emphasized that very few Christians are willing to support inner-city work. Many select churches which are safe physically as well as theologically, and it is a sad commentary on much modern-day evangelicalism that Christians tend to worship according to their social background.

Yet there is another area of preaching, outside our church buildings and beyond our pulpits, to which we need to address our attention. As we view the multitudes of the unreached we may well ask, 'How shall they hear without a preacher?' (Rom. 10:14). This surely implies that we must not limit preaching to sermons from the pulpit, but we must preach to the perishing wherever they are to be found. Where the lost are, there the preacher must also be, and there must be his 'pulpit'. This line of reasoning will help us to see that in door-to-door visitation, in city-centre outreach, or in the halls of residence of our colleges, we are just as much engaged in preaching as in our regular services. It will also prevent us from giving up such evangelistic efforts, even if they do not seem to bring people into our churches. Generally speaking we have been governed, consciously or otherwise, by a principle of pragmatism rather than by Scripture; but the fact is that whenever and wherever the Christian worker speaks for God to the lost, he is fulfilling his Lord's commission to preach the gospel to every creature.

The scene confronting us in our inner cities is one of twentieth-century paganism. It therefore requires a radical and pioneer approach, identical with that of the apostle Paul when he declared: 'Yea, so have I strived to preach the gospel, not where Christ was named, lest I should build upon another man's foundation: but as it is written, To whom he was not spoken of, they shall see: and they that have not heard shall understand' (Rom. 15:20-21). To this momentous statement we might add other words of Paul's: 'To preach the gospel in the regions beyond you, and not to boast in another man's line of things made ready to our hand'(2 Cor. 10:16).

We must be challenged to adopt a similar pioneer spirit. It was the burning ambition of Paul's life to go to those who had never heard. To 'strive' describes the effort he put into the proclamation of Christ in the unevangelized tracts of this world, and also the endurance required to accomplish it. John Bunyan, the immortal dreamer, shared the same strong conviction in the seventeenth century. He declared: 'My greatest desire in fulfilling my ministry was to get into the darkest places of the country, even among those people who were furthest off of profession . . . because I found my spirit did lean most after awakening and converting work, and the word that I carried did lean most that way also.'

THE CHURCH IN NEW AREAS

The preparation of workers

We come now to the practical side of inner-city gospel outreach. First, in addition to the witnessing done by our church members, there is need to set aside and prepare individuals as full-time pioneer evangelists. By 'pioneer' we mean that they are to be ready to speak to those who have never heard of the Lord Jesus as Saviour. It will be necessary for pastors and elders, and ultimately the church, to discern a man's gift both to preach to crowds and to get alongside individuals in all walks of life.

It is clear from the cases of both Paul and Bunyan that two of the prerequisites for an evangelist are earnestness and urgency. Certain individuals may therefore be disqualified by temperament from the office. Before appointing a man to such work, a church should en-quire whether he has been used to win souls for God. If he is to plan and execute inner-city evangelism, he must of necessity be a disciplined person, with consistent habits of prayer and study of God's Word. At the same time he must be a man who can speak plainly, avoiding evangelical jargon; one who is capable of starting where the people are, assuming that they know little of Christ and seeking to win them patiently to Him. In addition, he must be a person of initiative, able to cope with unexpected situations, and able also to cope with loneliness, possibly over long periods of time.

Siting of churches

As we survey the 'darkest places of the country', the church must be clearly guided to the areas God has chosen to evangelize. Paul's own experience reveals the danger of making the wrong choice. The Macedonian call (Acts 16:6-10) should teach us that cries for help should not go unheeded. We must be willing to hold back where God restrains, and to go forward as He constrains and commands. There must be a balance between spiritual openness to God's direction and spiritual listening to the cry of the people.

If the evangelist is to spearhead this advance into the virgin ter-ritory of our inner cities and housing estates, he must be constantly supported by the door-to-door visitation of church members. In time this will lead to the commencement of gospel meetings, where a hall, school or even a home may be used. As souls are won, new churches will be established in those places where God has chosen to work. We recall that 'the Lord appointed other seventy also, and sent them two and two before his face into every city and place, whither he himself would come' (Luke 10:1).

This is a wonderful way to begin working in an area. Another way is for an evangelist or pastor with a team of workers to seek to break into a new area. Ideally they will work outwards from the base of a local evangelical church. In addition to evening rallies, open-air meetings and door-to-door work, openings for the gospel can often be found through holding coffee mornings in homes or speaking in old people's homes, school assemblies and even classes.

Clearly, the same principles of evangelism apply to work on housing estates, but there are pitfalls to be avoided. For example, it would be unwise to erect a building until a church has really been established by the saving of souls. Again, one should avoid running such a work with the help of people who do not live on the estate, as this will cause the local residents never to see it as *their* church.

They will view the congregation almost as visitors from another planet, who 'land' on Sunday and disappear again until next week! (This may seem like a caricature, but there is some truth in it.)

We must begin by living there. This is far from easy; it demands a real sense of calling, and a certain degree of sacrifice. It involves the whole family, and it may affect the education of the children. It may also demand adaptation to a very different environment, possibly a violent one.

In some cases a different approach will have to be considered. We may need to do away with the idea of a separate congregation and ensure that local estates form part of the normal outreach of our churches. This would help to eliminate the tendency to make undesirable distinctions between believers by labelling them as estate or city Christians.

THE CHURCH IN ACTION

The place of prayer

The importance of prayer cannot be over-emphasized, because through it an entrance may be gained not only into people's homes but into their hearts. Prayer is needed both for doors of entrance and for doors of utterance. Paul could say to the Corinthians, 'For a great door and effectual is opened unto me, and there are many adversaries' (1 Cor. 16:9). On the other hand, he asked the believers at Colossae to pray that God would give to him and his companions 'a door of utterance' (Col. 4:3). Constant prayer is required that God will be with us as we advance into new areas. Our longing prayer should surely be:

> Breathe Thou abroad like morning air,
> Till hearts of stone begin to beat.

During one city mission, we set out after prayer to do door-to-door visitation. As I approached the first door, I felt a terrible sense of oppression and a real reluctance to embark on this visit. The young woman who opened the door told me that the man she lived with was going to leave her because she refused to rob a sick old man she was nursing. Suddenly she said, 'Could you get me a Bible?' Sensing her need, I invited her to the service that evening. She was saved that night, not only from sin but from her planned suicide the next day. The man left her, but God did not. When the old man was removed to hospital later that week, she insisted that I visit him. I was indeed humbled when she took the sick man's face between her hands and said to him, 'I have brought a man of God

83

to see you.' There within the space of a few days one witnessed a life saved from suicide, a soul saved from hell, and an evangelist born!

Running a 'rescue shop'

Today many church-going people have rejected the invitation to Christ's 'marriage supper'; they too have begun to 'make excuse' (Luke 14:18). It is surely time to obey the Lord's command, 'Go out quickly into the streets and lanes of the city and bring in hither the poor, and the maimed, and the halt, and the blind' (v.21).

Dr F. B. Meyer, the founder under God of the church where I now minister, held a prayer meeting in the church every Saturday night which was attended by several hundred people. After they had pleaded with God for the needs of the people, a 'rescue squad' would go in search of the needy and the outcasts, seeking to lead them to Christ and, if possible, helping them in practical ways. Before he embarked upon his work of evangelization (not of an inner city, but of the interior of a continent), C.T. Studd, the converted cricketer, said:

> *Some wish to live within the sound*
> *Of church or chapel bell:*
> *I want to run a rescue shop*
> *Within a yard of hell.*

It is time we did just that. Every night in the centre of our cities you will find young people setting out for sinful enjoyment in night clubs or discos, or hanging about aimlessly with nothing to do. I can testify that however cold the night, however inopportune the moment or however inappropriate the place may seem to be, God is always there. What is needed is that a group of people who have prayerfully sought the Lord beforehand should go out and stand on that city patch and speak for Him. Many more have heard the gospel in one-to-one conversations in this way than have been reached inside the church building. The essential requirements are love, the ability to listen, and sheer God-given endurance. We have visited our city centre in this way twice weekly for over six years. Even if results are few, it demonstrates the fact that God cares — and did not Christ seek the lost sheep *'till he found it'* (Luke 15:4)? Alternatively, some can perhaps be brought back to the church coffee bar where, after informal conversations and refreshments, the life-changing gospel is preached. I also know of one evangelist in the Midlands who preaches in the open air at midday in four cities weekly throughout the year.

84

THE CHURCH AND THE NEEDY

In our inner cities unemployment is a constant problem. To help the unemployed, a coffee bar could be opened on a regular basis. It would need to be manned by a dedicated staff who could 'sit where they sit'. Here in the city also are the drop-outs, the alcoholics, the outcasts of society; their numbers are growing, and their average age decreasing. Hostels too are needed to help the many homeless people; these should be linked to city churches and financed by them. In our church, a Christian lady has a home for girls in need. Here Christian young people can befriend them and bring the gospel to them. Similarly, we have a house for Christian young men, and we encourage them to use it as a base for evangelism and for building bridges between the neighbourhood and the church.

There are many categories of needy women in our inner cities today: deserted wives living in loneliness and, sadly, battered wives too. How easy it is just to pass by on the other side! To gain access to these people, a lady worker is needed. She is needed too to reach those other pathetic women, the prostitutes. Great wisdom is needed here, for behind the prostitutes are men who organize that traffic. All needy women, however, can be encouraged to attend 'Mum Take a Break' clubs or church coffee bars, and thus come to hear the everlasting gospel. Personally I know of no other way to reach these various women and show them that God is love and that He still cares.

In inner-city work we often meet people who ask for money, but in many cases they intend to spend it on alcohol rather than on necessities. Food can be given to them, and if there are Christian hostels to which they would be willing to go, they can be directed there. In our church we take an offering after the Lord's Supper to support this benevolent work and, where possible, to help those who are in real need.

Some inner-city churches find running their own play-schools an excellent means of outreach to children and their mothers. Midweek Bible clubs, holiday Bible weeks and, of course, our own Sunday schools are all very good ways of reaching the ever-increasing number of children who have never heard the gospel. We shall go on to consider the question of ethnic minorities, but we would draw attention here to the fact that many of our children are brainwashed by the teaching of comparative religion in their schools, where Christianity is often greatly down-graded.[2] Some Christian children are even looked down upon if they do not enter into the festivities of non-Christian religions, which become an integral part of school activities at certain times of the year.

Who is the inner-city worker who does not sometimes feel like giving up? Yet there are times when God breaks in! Some years ago, when riots had just finished in the area where our church is situated, we were due to start a week's mission. Night after night, up to a hundred young people would be crowded around the tables of the coffee bar, filling in questionnaires about Christianity. The noise would be deafening. But when the message was given, they listened in an awesome silence which could only have been created by the Spirit, and the conversations that followed would sometimes go on until midnight. That mission could not end after a week, but continued from August to November, when violence compelled us to close the coffee bar for a period.

Yet, having considered all these ways of reaching the lost in our cities, we still recognize the need to 'run a rescue shop within a yard of hell'. We need a place right where the people are, a place which enables believers to take them off the streets and bring them into an informal, loving atmosphere where Christ can be presented to them, a place to which people can come at any time. Here, besides making cups of tea and coffee available, it may be possible to have a well-stocked bookstall on the premises. In such welcoming surroundings it should be feasible to run evangelistic coffee mornings and lunch-time meetings for the workers who throng our inner cities. This should be seen not as a new mission separate from the church, but rather as a further means of showing Christian compassion, reaching the people where they are and plucking the brands out of the burning. To those engaged in such work comes the reassurance, 'Be not afraid . . . no man shall set upon thee to hurt thee: for I have much people in this city' (Acts 18:9,10).

THE CHURCH AND ETHNIC MINORITIES

In our inner cities we are now faced with a phenomenon which the church in Britain has never had to face on the same scale before — a multiracial and a multi-religious society. As Christians we must rejoice that the Lord has brought the world to our doorstep. What an opportunity lies before us! Not even Wesley, Whitefield or Spurgeon could ever have conceived of it. Some churches are fearful of the inroads that Islam is making into our land; but we must rather seize upon this situation as a providential opportunity for evangelism. The city where I have the privilege of ministering has the largest Gujarati population outside India. We are aware that for years our politicians and city planners have called for integration, but anyone who has spent a few years working in such a society realizes that to dream of this is naive, to say the least. We are faced with people who not only have different religions and languages, but who also belong to a totally different culture. The only integration possible is into Christ, and that is not going to happen overnight.

I believe that we need to understand and respect the cultures of these different peoples, and we should never give the impression that the gospel demands a Western life-style. Christianity does not destroy culture, but removes its barriers. Grace will gradually sift from our different backgrounds everything that is alien to the Word of God.

How shall we approach the task? We must go again to the streets and take the love of Christ to people's doors. We must not think that language barriers are insurmountable; they are not. But when we seek to reach people of other religions and cultures we greatly need the guidance of Christian nationals, or else retired or retiring missionaries who have worked amongst such people in their own lands.

Some have sought to establish Asian, West Indian and Chinese churches in our cities. This seems a natural and an easy solution, but in my view it completely ignores the idea that the church is 'all one in Christ Jesus', a fellowship in which there is 'neither Jew nor Greek . . . neither bond nor free' (Gal. 3:28). The church on earth should reflect heaven, where there are people of every tongue and tribe and nation worshipping *together*. Our aim must be to seek to establish a multiracial church, because we are heading towards a multiracial heaven. The church should be international because the gospel is international. Has not Christ commanded us, 'Go ye into all the *world*, and preach . . .?' Dare we divide up believers whom Christ has joined in one body? It is surely unthinkable! Did not Christ pray that the world might see that we are one?

Yet we must be realistic. Language and cultural barriers, even the natural suspicion and colour prejudice harboured by some Christians, may keep people of other nationalities from entering our churches. We must build bridges between us. For example, it is good to have outreach meetings for Chinese people and for those from the Indian subcontinent. Christians of the same ethnic background can then welcome their fellow countrymen, and they may even like to prepare some of their favourite dishes. The hymns and the Scriptures should on these occasions be in their own language, and it is essential that the preaching of the gospel be paramount. Church members could visit the homes of these often lonely people, and also invite them to their own homes. It would be an excellent development if more English-speaking Christians were

87

led by God to serve Him in this way. Christian teachers could arrange to take English classes in homes for those who know little or no English. Such people often need help also in filling in complex forms and overcoming other problems of settling in our land. It is good to encourage their children and young people, who are being educated in English, to attend our church Sunday schools and young people's activities.

We have in our membership an 80-year-old missionary and his wife, who began their service in China in 1931 and, since 1977, have been working with the Chinese in Leicester. They have brought the gospel to those who work in restaurants and take-away shops, and they hold a weekly Bible class for them in their own language. Sometimes the missionary goes to court to help those who get into trouble with the police. Recently I had the pleasure of baptizing several believers: apart from one Scot, they were all Indian or Chinese. The five Chinese were restaurant workers who spoke very little English; they were all former Buddhists and had been involved in ancestor and spirit worship. These are by no means all the converts whom God in His mercy has given us.

The Asians from the Indian subcontinent have a similar weekly meeting which is also attended by British workers. This is a wonderful ministry, not only for missionaries retiring from abroad, but also for new missionaries who want to gain some experience in Britain first. Some missionaries are hindered from returning to their fields of service because of visa difficulties with governments or problems at home. Yet here in our inner cities there is a mission field open to them — indeed there may be several within a mile radius of our church buildings — Buddhists, Muslims, Hindus and Sikhs to be won for Christ. Not long ago a converted Sikh went to Bible College from our church and was called to serve among his own Punjabi-speaking people in Southall. In addition, an Anglo-Indian man in his forties, with a wife and two teenage sons, was called to full-time service; he has completed three years of Bible College training and has a burden to reach Muslims in Britain.

I sometimes wonder what William Carey would have thought about it all. He lived in Leicester, and he left these shores to devote his life to the service of God in India. I have no doubt that his advice to our churches today would be identical with that which he gave in his own day: 'Expect great things from God; attempt great things for God.'

NOTES

1 The early ministry of Martyn Lloyd-Jones during the inter-war years of economic depression in South Wales should also be recalled. It is recounted by Iain Murray in *D. Martyn Lloyd-Jones: The First Forty Years, 1899-1939* (Banner of Truth, 1982). Chalmers's work in Edinburgh and, later on, in Glasgow, was not evangelistic in any narrow sense. His vision was also to establish what today might be called a diaconal ministry of social concern.

2 Fred Hughes makes some suggestions in his chapter about the kind of action Christian parents may undertake in relation to their children's schools.

QUESTIONS FOR DISCUSSION

a) 'Lord, what wilt thou have me to do?' (Acts 9:6). What ways can we use daily to *reach the unreached* outside the walls of our churches?

b) Jesus said, 'Let us go into the next towns, that I may preach there also' (Mark 1:38). How can we determine the next town where God wants to work?

c) C. T. Studd wanted 'to run a rescue shop within a yard of hell'. How would you go about setting up a rescue shop in your inner city?

d) 'How shall they hear without a preacher?' (Rom. 10:14). How can we discern, train and set aside pioneers from our congregations?

FURTHER READING

Roy Joslin's *Urban Harvest* (Evangelical Press, 1982) is a history of the attitudes of city dwellers and an account of present-day work in an inner-city church. He makes suggestions about methods of approach. *The Young Woman Who Lived in a Shoe* by Elizabeth Braund (Prisca Books, 1984) describes her work among the boys of Upper Clapham. The history and present-day work of the London City Mission is described by Phyllis Thompson in *To the Heart of the City* (Hodder & Stoughton, n.d.). A video of the work of the Mission can be obtained from the LCM at 175 Tower Bridge Road, London SE1 2AL. A discussion of the theological issues posed by witness in the inner city can be read in Roger Greenway's edited collection, *Discipling the City* (Baker Book House, 1979).

6

Work and Unemployment

GERALLT WYN DAVIES

Rich and poor countries throughout the world are currently experiencing persistent high levels of unemployment. The scale of the problem is so great that in 1982 the International Labour Organization estimated that one billion new jobs would have to be created in order to obtain global full employment by the year 2,000.

In the United Kingdom over the last 25 years the working population has risen by nearly three million. This increase is due partly to a growth in the number of people of working age (16-60/64), and partly to a rise in the 'activity' or participation rates, that is, in the number of people (such as married women) who wish to work. The employment situation in the United Kingdom during the 1980s may be summarized as follows:[1]

United Kingdom: constitution of working population

Status	Total/Percentage		Trend
Full-time employment	16,000,000	(53.3%)	Decreasing
Part-time employment	5,000,000	(16.7%)	Increasing
Unpaid domestic workers	3,500,000	(11.7%)	Decreasing
Self-employed	2,500,000	(8.3%)	Increasing
Unemployed	3,000,000	(10.0%)	Increasing
TOTAL	30,000,000	(100.0%)	

These long-term trends may be illustrated by what took place during the period 1977-84, when the population of working age rose by 1.3 million, while the employed labour force fell by 791,000, resulting in a rise of 1.58 million in unemployment. This rise in unemployment would have been considerably larger, were it not for the following factors: a rise of nearly 500,000 in the number of self-employed persons; a reduction in activity rates as more people took early retirement, and the fact that fewer married women

91

sought employment because of the poor prospects of obtaining a job, while many others accepted part-time employment. In addition, various government training and job creation schemes removed some 600,000 young people from the unemployment register (at least temporarily) at any one time, and revised definitions of employment excluded some thousands from official statistics. It must also be remembered that unemployment rates varied by over 10 per cent between the worst affected region (Northern Ireland) and that least affected (south-east England).[2]

Growth in the working population is not in itself an insurmountable problem. During 1930-39 the working population grew by 11 per cent but unemployment was halved, and between 1932 and 1937 employment rose by 2.6 million. Growth in the industrial sector and changes in monetary, mercantile and military policy enabled the increased working population to be absorbed into jobs. Furthermore, the current growth in the UK population is lower than in the USA and in the majority of industrialized countries.[3]

However, it is generally agreed that the variables which affect levels of employment and unemployment are complex. They include economic, technological, financial and social factors, and the interaction between them as well as their durability means that there are no simple solutions. These factors are not in themselves new. Mavor, writing in the 1900s, states that 'An excess of labourers seeking employment may of itself produce, through a series of reactions, the phenomenon of unemployment', and goes on to list, among other causative factors, the rate of interest, scarcity of raw materials and changing market forces, as well as 'changes in tariffs, in technical processes (as in the displacement of hand labour by machinery and the substitution of one machine for another), or in transportation routes'.[4] It may be argued that during the thirties these factors (eventually) interacted favourably, as they did again in the fifties and sixties, and that there was also the political will to find solutions and to give the reduction of unemployment a high priority.

The situation is different now. The working population has increased and is largely dependent upon paid employment in urban conurbations. Technological innovation, particularly in the microelectronic and computer fields, feeds on itself in ways not previously experienced, and this makes for rapid and pervasive changes, which are bringing about a long-term, dramatic reduction both in the number of jobs available and in the nature of work itself. Competition between companies and nations to gain markets for their products and services fuels the drive to reduce labour costs and to improve quality by lessening dependence upon human skill and effort. At the same time, the fiscal policies pursued by governments have a substantial effect on the level of demand for goods and services — and, consequently, on employment levels. Such factors, in combination, are formidable obstacles, not simply to the reduction of current levels of unemployment, but even to the retention of current levels of employment.

It is also important to remember that the motivation to find solutions to unemployment and the choice as to which solutions should be pursued depend in no small measure on the role work is seen to fulfil in the life of human beings, and on the value which is placed on human life. If work is seen as an acquired habit or compulsion, reinforced by social values and economic conventions, then one solution is to re-educate people to manage unlimited leisure, and to change social values and economic conventions so that people can enjoy non-employment without guilt or financial hardship. If, however, involvement in daily work is perceived as an essential condition of physical and mental well-being, then a reconsideration of the concept of work, the creation of work and the sharing of available work is the course of action which should be given high priority. A third alternative is to regard the unemployment of a substantial number of the population as the regrettable but unavoidable price of progress, to provide financial support so as to minimize the resultant material hardship, and to hope that the problem will resolve itself over a period of time.

WORK IN A SECULAR SOCIETY

In a secular society in which the majority have faith in nothing apart from the material universe, work assumes a particular importance for many. It becomes their main source of purpose and value in life. For them unemployment, and even retirement, means the loss not simply of their livelihood but of all worthwhile status and meaning. Many secular writers, therefore, when referring to 'the dignity of work', go on to describe that dignity in instrumental terms, such as its value in enabling a person to support a family and to have a sense of purpose and status in life, rather than in terms of the intrinsic quality of work itself. However, it is by no means universal for a high value to be placed on work. For example, David Jenkins states that 'the distaste for work is so general and so widespread that one intriguing question arises quite noticeably: Is work necessary?'[5] Many people, from doctors to dustmen, complain about their jobs and say that they wish financial necessity did not require them to work. It may be argued, therefore, that as current advances in technology enable us to create sufficient wealth without human effort, it will be desirable to develop a society in which people are freed from dependence upon work for their livelihoods and for their sense of purpose and status. In such a society leisure and voluntary work would become central activities through which people would find fulfilment.

It is important to note that while the Scriptures emphasize the need for people to work (as we shall see later), they also warn of the danger of work assuming a false, over-important role in life and in society as a whole. In preparing the Israelites to enter Canaan to establish the thriving and secure society He had promised them, God warned the people not to let success and affluence lead them into ill-founded self-reliance and forgetting Him:

> Take heed lest you forget the Lord, who brought you out of the land of Egypt, out of the house of bondage . . . Take heed lest you forget the Lord your God, by not keeping his commandments . . . lest, when you have eaten and are full . . . then your heart be lifted up, and you forget the Lord your God . . . Beware lest you say in your heart, 'My power and the might of my hand have gotten me this wealth.'
>
> Deuteronomy 6:12; 8:11,12,14,17 (RSV)

However, the seductive power of secure affluence is strong, and the Israelites had few resources with which to resist. The warnings were strongly reinforced, therefore, through the institution of sabbath observance. The seventh day was to be 'the sabbath of the Lord', in which no work was to be done (Deut. 5:12-15). This was not simply an act of religious devotion, but one of confession that the source of true meaning, purpose and progress in their lives was God, and that their future within the land was dependent upon their relationship with Him. Life was at His disposal and not theirs![6]

Every seventh year the sabbath principle was to apply to the land. After six years of tilling, sowing and reaping, 'then shall the land keep a sabbath . . . in the seventh year . . . thou shalt neither sow thy field, nor prune thy vineyard' (Lev. 25:2-4 AV). Thus these Israelite slaves-become-landowners are reminded that the land is a gift to which they have no inherent right, but it will remain a guaranteed possession as long as they continue to observe the terms of the covenant:

> Therefore it shall come to pass, that as all good things are come upon you, which the Lord your God promised you; so shall the Lord bring upon you all evil things . . . when ye have transgressed the covenant of the Lord your God, which he commanded you, and have gone and serv-

ed other gods . . . and ye shall perish quickly from off the good land
which he hath given unto you.   Joshua 23:15-16 (AV)

Finally, every fiftieth year there was a year of jubilee. 'The sanctions of the Sabbatical year were enforced. In addition, property
reverted to its original owners, debts were remitted, and Hebrews
who had been enslaved for debt were released. It was a time of
thanksgiving and an occasion for the exercise of faith that God
would provide food (Lev. 25:8 etc.).'[7] The sabbath was therefore a
powerful means of keeping the people faithful to the covenant and
standards of God in their relationship to the land, to their own lives
and to their fellow men. Its observance is their acknowledgment
that society does not finally depend on trading and toiling, but on
God and their faithfulness to Him. Generations later, Amos
understood that the abandonment of a sabbath-keeping spirit was
at the root of the nation's degeneration into a self-securing, ex-
ploiting people who were about to lose their land as God's judgment came upon them:

> Hear this, O you who would swallow up . . . the needy, even to make
> the poor of the land to fail, saying, When will the new moon festival be
> past, that we may sell grain? And the sabbath, that we may offer wheat
> for sale, making the ephah small, and the shekel great, and falsifying the
> scales by deceit? . . . The Lord hath sworn . . . Surely I will never forget
> any of their deeds. Shall not the land tremble on this account, and every
> one mourn who dwells in it?   Amos 8:4-5,7-8

The centrality of the sabbath-keeping spirit to the well-being of
societies and individuals is also vividly stated in the first chapter of
Paul's letter to the Roman church, where he exposes the inevitable
consequences of a failure to glorify God as God. The consistent
theme of Scripture, therefore, is that the abandonment of God
always and everywhere results in confusion, moral declension and
dehumanization. An acknowledgment of the truth of this is essential to a right understanding of our society and age. The secularization of our age, in both capitalist and communist societies, has inevitably involved the abandonment of a sabbath-keeping spirit and
led to a denial of the authenticity of meaning and values derived
from God. The results are as inevitable and dehumanizing as they
were for Israel and Rome.

One of these results is that economic work comes to be regarded
as the key determinant of progress, and the value placed on people
is measured according to the contribution they make to that process. In other words, societies that abandon the sabbath-keeping

95

spirit in the end always overturn the biblical principle that 'work is made for man' by operating as if 'man is made for work'. Economic work is then elevated so as to become the most important of human activities, either because it is regarded as a key determinant of affluence (as in capitalist societies), or because it is perceived as a key determinant of history (as in communist societies). When this happens, man comes to be valued primarily only as a worker, and so he may justifiably be required to contribute to the greater good of the society to which he belongs in ways and on terms determined by what is expedient for that society.[8]

By the same token, when he becomes a non-worker in such a society — whether unemployed, disabled or retired — man may be regarded no longer as an asset but as a liability, and economic progress and the motivation and reward of the employed must take precedence over his well-being. Further, the impact of labour-saving technologies and competitive international trade increasingly render the employment of people an uneconomic way of creating wealth. While this trend persists, and financial objectives such as the reduction of inflation remain government priorities, the continuing long-term unemployment even of a substantial minority is likely to be regarded as an unfortunate but necessary price to pay for the continued security and affluence of the majority.

> There is a strong conflict of interest between those who are in employment and those who are unemployed, which the unions are unwilling to recognize, for the unions are, in fact, primarily financed by those who are in employment. Somehow it is difficult to see shop stewards and union officials backing away from employers, begging, 'No, please, no more money — give it to the needy, the poor, the jobless.'[9]

If governments are also able to convince people that the state has limited discretion in influencing employment levels, the pressure brought to bear on the state is unlikely to be sufficient for the reduction of unemployment to be treated as a matter of great urgency. (A White Paper published in 1985 presented arguments along these lines.[10] It referred to the complexity of factors like those we have already mentioned, to vagaries in the labour market and to irresponsible wage increases, all of which were said to reduce what the Government could do to reduce unemployment.) When human life itself is ambiguously valued, there is no intrinsic reason why a pragmatic, secular society, given to the pursuit of progress, should give high priority to alleviating what is, by and large, the unseen despair of its jobless minority.

96

THE CHRISTIAN DOCTRINE OF WORK

The Christian teaching regarding human nature and work differs radically from the dominant secular view. Christianity presents the only way to release men from a twentieth-century form of slavery in which 'meaningless and apostate man finds himself reduced by his own science and technology to a cog in the great machine of nature and society'.[11]

It does so by maintaining, firstly, that *human beings are created in the image of God,* and that God has delegated to man

> the authority to manage or have dominion over the physical world. This is a privilege because it puts man at the head of the created world . . . Man has been created with an urge to control and harness the resources of nature in the interests of the common good, but he is subject to his accountability to God as trustee to preserve and care for it (Gen. 1:26).[12]

While man is, therefore, part of the created order, he is also unique: he alone is made in the image of God; he alone is given authority over the created order, and he alone has the capacity of thought and invention to undertake such a stewardship and be accountable for it.

Secondly, Christian teaching maintains that, as a being created in the image of God, *man through working finds fulfilment which cannot be obtained through any other activity.* The Bible refers to God working, for example, in creation. Jesus Christ undertook manual, social and intellectual tasks, such as carpentry, healing and teaching. Man made in the image of God shares that fundamental need to work.

> The Bible nowhere suggests that working is the result of the Fall. Man was given both manual (gardening) and intellectual (naming the animals) tasks before the Fall, and it is through these natural activities that man's strengths and skills are developed, nature's resources realized, man satisfied and God glorified (Gen. 1:26-31).[13]

However, while work remains an irreplaceable means of human development and fulfilment, what was intended to be a pleasurable activity is now accompanied by frustrations and failures. As a consequence of rebelling against God, man incurred judgment which affected all his relationships.

> Because thou hast hearkened unto the voice of thy wife, and hast eaten of the tree, of which I commanded thee, saying, Thou shalt not eat of it: cursed is the ground for thy sake; in sorrow shalt thou eat of it all the days of thy life.
> Genesis 3:17 (AV)

97

The creation itself is affected by man's rebellion, and people are not only at odds with one another but at odds with themselves because, divorced from God, they do not know who they are or why they are on earth.

> And whatever my eyes desired I kept not from them; I withheld not my heart from any pleasure, for my heart rejoiced in all my labour, and this was my portion and reward for all my toil. Then I looked on all that my hands had done and the labour I had spent in doing it, and behold, all was vanity and searching for wind and feeding on it, and there was no profit under the sun.   Ecclesiastes 2:10-11

Thirdly, *the Christian regard for man's uniqueness requires that work should constitute 'meaningful activity'.* This means activity which is consistent with man's nature and contributes to the creation purposes already stated. Such activity will include much, but by no means all, paid work. For example, assembly-line jobs which require operators to undertake simple, repetitive tasks which could be just as well undertaken by trained monkeys do not constitute meaningful activity. On the other hand, the work of a housewife and mother, or voluntary social work, in which the whole being is involved in the service of others, certainly comes into this category. It is important to note also that all such work constitutes a vocation or calling. The distinction that is often drawn between 'sacred' and 'secular' work is not biblical. Work is never to be regarded as a neutral activity; it is undertaken either in obedience or in disobedience to God's leading or calling. A particular job is therefore right or wrong for an individual Christian according to whether or not it is undertaken in obedience to God's call and is carried out in a way that acknowledges and honours Him. The parables of the rich farmer (Luke 12:16-21) and the unjust steward (Luke 16:1-12) both spell out the dangers of living life in 'sacred' and 'secular' compartments, where God is relegated to a secondary place in the main activities and interests of life. Other scriptures also are quite specific in their instructions about the conduct of daily work. For example:

> Servants, obey in everything those who are your earthly masters, not only when their eyes are on you, as pleasers of men, but in simplicity of purpose [with all your heart] because of your reverence for the Lord . . . Whatever may be your task, work at it heartily . . . as [something done] for the Lord and not for men . . . Masters, [on your part] deal with your slaves justly and fairly, knowing that also you have a Master in heaven.
> Colossians 3:22-23; 4:1

Fourthly, *Christians are commanded to work in order to support themselves and their families as well as to have to give to those in need.* In the words of the apostle Paul:

> Let the thief steal no more, but rather let him be industrious, making an honest living with his own hands, so that he may be able to give to those in need.   Ephesians 4:28

The apostle John goes further, and questions the authenticity of any man's Christian profession if he fails to assist a fellow Christian in need when he is in a position to do so:

> But if anyone has this world's goods . . . and sees his brother . . . in need, yet closes his heart of compassion against him, how can the love of God live . . . in him?   1 John 3:17

However, the use of available resources to help the needy is not only an exhortation addressed to individuals, but is frequently the subject of instruction (2 Cor. 8:13-14) or commendation (1 Thess. 4:9) in the apostle Paul's letters to churches.

> The New Testament evidence indicates that the expression of brotherly love in regular giving was widespread in the early church, such ministry taking different forms according to the circumstances, but always incorporating the same motivation and principles as are seen in what has been called 'the Jerusalem experiment' (Acts 2:44-47; 4:32-35). Its essence was the formation of a common fund, which was maintained by voluntary contributions and used to meet the needs of all members of the church. In Acts 2, all members contributed such as they had, and the well-endowed sold their properties in order to make the proceeds available for the common good. Such action does not appear to have been a condition of church membership, but was a common, voluntary expression of fellowship and love. Later on, in Acts 6:1-6, deacons were appointed in order to effect a fair distribution of aid, and this is significant 'as the first example of that delegation of administrative and social responsibilities to those of appropriate character and gifts, which was to become typical of the Gentile churches, and the recognition of such duties as part of the ministry of Christ'.[15,16]

Implications of the Christian doctrine of work

There are two implications deriving from what has been said above which are particularly important for Christians living in a secular age. First, a right understanding of the teaching regarding work will enrich their own lives, leading as it does to the conviction that God desires to guide and act through each Christian's life, whatever vocation He calls them to undertake. This transforms everyday work into purposeful activity (which is the meaning of the Greek word *ergazomai* used by Paul in Ephesians 4:28) in spite of all its frustrations and disappointments. Christians should have the confidence to seek guidance about what work to undertake, and to expect and pray that God will minister 'salt' and 'light' through them as they seek to serve Him in the particular situations into which He leads them.

> What distinguishes the Christian worker from the unbeliever is the sense of mission he demonstrates in his labours. The housewife who placed this sign over the kitchen sink had the right idea of her particular calling: 'Divine service held here three times daily.' The message of Christ's Lordship to the worker is simply this: 'God wants *you* . . . in *your* job.'[16]

The second implication derives from the New Testament emphasis on the need for Christians, both as individuals and churches, to exercise good stewardship in utilizing the fruits of their labour (whether these be money, position, knowledge or skills) to assist those who are in need. In so far as the unemployed are concerned, it is important in a secular society to propagate the Christian teaching regarding the uniqueness of man and the irreplaceable role of work in human life, for it provides convincing reasons why the creation and reorganization of work to alleviate unemployment and its miserable effects should be given the highest priority by societies and governments. While most of the debates about unemployment are couched in economic and financial terms, such as 'the cost to the country' and 'wasted resources', research findings in the 1930s as well as in recent years[17,18] have consistently substantiated the Christian contention that the main and heavy cost of unemployment is borne by the individuals who experience it, especially those who experience long-term, enforced unemployment. Man created in the image of God is too important for this; he is not meant to be treated as a means to an end, to be used and discarded according to economic convenience.

When faced with the scale and complexity of the current problems of employment and unemployment, and with the need to rethink the role and organization of work in our society, the temptation even for people of conviction and goodwill is to feel helpless. However, there *are* practical ways in which individuals and churches can and should (and in some cases do) assist unemployed persons in their neighbourhoods.

First, the effects of unemployment need to be alleviated through both material and moral support. Since most unemployed people suffer from a sense of failure and hopelessness, however, the giving of such support is a sensitive matter, calling for much wisdom and grace on the part of individuals and churches. Nevertheless, helping to meet the needs of those near at hand out of the abundance with which they may have been provided is the readiest practical way in which the 7 million or so church members in the United Kingdom can demonstrate personal, loving care for those who are unemployed (2 Cor. 8:14).

Secondly, unemployment itself needs to be reduced through increased training and job opportunities. This also needs much wisdom, since what is provided must be real, meaningful activity; if it is merely something fabricated and temporary, it often serves to accentuate a sense of inadequacy and dependence in those it is meant to help. However, that effective action is possible has been demonstrated by such bodies as Church Action with the Unemployed, which recently published details of 100 different projects undertaken by individuals or churches, claiming that these represented 'less than one in ten of those which churches had been involved in'.[19] The projects published range from a church-based neighbourhood care scheme, manned by nine people who were unemployed, to a print shop serving voluntary groups and employing seven people. More than 75 per cent of the projects listed are funded by the Manpower Services Commission. However, each church must consider carefully what is within its capacity, and must ensure there is sufficient commitment to see a project through once it is initiated. To abandon it after having started is more damaging than not to start at all.

Finally, there is need for political action in order to emphasize the responsibility of governments to work for the well-being of all the population, and especially to re-examine the whole concept of work and its organization. The irreplaceable contribution work makes to individual and family well-being, and the almost certain long-term shortage of jobs as they are conceived of in present-day terms, make such re-examination vital. If changes are to be made which are sufficient to eradicate long-term unemployment in this country and the widespread endemic unemployment that exists in many other countries, it will entail rethinking and reforming current concepts of the 'working day' and the 'working week', the labour market and its operation, and the work/pay relationship. Not long ago the Charter for Jobs was established, with three former Prime Ministers as patrons, in order to campaign for decisive action by the Government to reduce unemployment.[20] Such pressure groups should receive Christian support. Individuals and Christian organizations should also ask members of Parliament and of the Lords to take action. An example of such action would be the establishment of a Royal Commission to undertake a thorough examination of the future of work, and of ways in which it might be organized so as to ensure that every person who desires to work has the opportunity to do so.

Not all of these actions will be practicable or necessary in every situation. However, since current high levels of unemployment are likely to continue for the foreseeable future, individuals and churches have an obligation to consider how they should respond in seeking to alleviate the consequent needs.

Of course, reasons for not helping needy neighbours can easily be found, as the parable of the good Samaritan shows so clearly (Luke 10:30-37). But if a sceptical world is to be convinced that Christianity is more than sentimental make-believe, it must see the power of Christian love demonstrated in action as well as in truth, and this means seeking out and meeting the needs of the unemployed, the weak and the deprived (1 John 3:18).

NOTES

1 C. Handy, *The Future of Work* (Blackwells, 1984).
2 Lloyds Bank *Economic Bulletin* (May, 1987).
3 D. Metcalf and J. Nickell, 'Jobs and Pay', *Midland Bank Review* (Spring 1985).
4 J. Mavor, 'Employment' in *Encyclopaedia of Religion and Ethics* ed. by J. Hastings (T. & T. Clark, 1912).
5 D. Jenkins, *Job Power: Blue and White Collar Democracy* (Heinemann, 1973).
6 W. Brueggemann, *The Land* (SPCK, 1978).
7 D. Freeman, 'Sabbatical Year' in *Illustrated Bible Dictionary* (Inter-Varsity Press, 1980).
8 J. Robertson, *What Comes After Full Employment?* (The Other Economic Summit, 1984).
9 W. Robbins, 'Reduction of Working Hours — The Trends', *Digest of the Institute of Personnel Management* (December 1979).
10 *Employment: The Challenge to the Nation* (Department of Employment, March 1985).
11 F. Schaeffer, *The Church at the End of the Twentieth Century* (Hodder & Stoughton, 1975).
12 B. Griffiths, *The Creation of Wealth* (Hodder & Stoughton, 1984).
13 G. W. Davies, *The Christian, the Church and Daily Work* (Evangelical Press of Wales, 1984).
14 A. F. Walls, 'Deacon' in *New Bible Dictionary* ed. by J. D. Douglas (Inter-Varsity Press, 1962).
15 G. W. Davies, *The Christian, the Church and Daily Work.*
16 C. F. H. Henry, *Aspects of Christian Social Ethics* (Eerdmans, 1964).
17 R. Smith, *Unemployment and Health* (Oxford University Press, 1987).
18 R. Harrison, 'The Demoralising Experience of Unemployment', *Department of Employment Gazette* (April 1976).

19 *Action on Unemployment* (Church Action with the Unemployed, 1984).
20 Charter for Jobs Council, *We Can Cut Unemployment* (Charter for Jobs, 1985).

QUESTIONS FOR DISCUSSION

a) Prepare a brief discussion paper setting out biblical reasons why individual Christians and/or churches should act to help the unemployed, and propose actions suitable for your church/study group.

b) Ask each member of a study group to search out Scriptures which guide Christians regarding their conduct at work, and use an overhead projector or flip-chart to summarize the principles and their practical implications.

c) Explore the New Testament teaching regarding the Sabbath as well as the Old Testament teaching outlined in this chapter, and work out what this means for Sunday worship, work, witness and leisure.

d) What differences do you envisage would result from using the biblical concept of 'meaningful activity' to reorganize the totality of work available in our society?

FURTHER READING

Action on Unemployment (Church Action with the Unemployed, 1984). This details 100 projects with unemployed people.

Archbishop of Canterbury's Commission on Urban Priority Areas, *Faith in the City: A Call for Action by Church and Nation* (Church House Publishing, 1985).

H. F. R. Catherwood, *The Christian in Industrial Society* (Tyndale Press, 1966). The author seeks to establish Christian standards by applying Christian doctrine to different aspects of life in an industrial society.

W. Green, *The Christian and Unemployment* (Mowbray, 1982). A parish study guide towards a new understanding of work, with Bible references and questions for group discussion. It has 45 pages and 15 chapters, and includes a section on 'Sources of Information and Support'.

Brian Griffiths, *The Creation of Wealth* (Hodder & Stoughton, 1984). An exposition of the market economy, and the application to it of biblical principles.

Charles Handy, *The Future of Work* (Blackwells, 1984). A thorough examination of the prospects and issues, based on the assumption that man is a compulsive worker.

Richard Smith, *Unemployment and Health* (Oxford University Press, 1987). An important study of the relationship between unemployment and health and a consideration of the implications.

D. J. Winwood, *Ways to Work with the young Unemployed* (Methodist Association of Youth Clubs, 1981). A useful 12-page guide for a church looking for different ways to support and help unemployed young people.

7

Christian Concern for Education

FRED HUGHES

In this chapter I want first to consider the importance of education, and the nature of education in our society.[1] Then I propose to examine the implications of Christian doctrine for education, and seek to clarify what Christians should seek and how they should seek it. Finally, I should like to comment briefly on church schools and Christian schools.

THE BIG WORLD OF EDUCATION

There can hardly be a person in Britain who has no relative involved in school. In January 1986, nine and a half million children in the United Kingdom were attending school (over 600,000 of them in independent schools),[2] and that means that a lot of families are involved. And when we consider that most if not all of us rub shoulders with children and young people daily in our streets, shops, parks, buses and trains, we can see plainly that in one way or another we are all affected by what schools are doing to the children of our land.

That is one way of saying that education is important. It is not some small, incidental aspect of society which most of us have little or no responsibility to consider, but an aspect that is important enough to warrant the attention of large numbers of Christians.

How then can we describe the schools in our land? It is risky to generalize, as schools vary a great deal. Some have modern buildings: some do not. Some are large: others are small. Some have a wide age range (e.g. 4-11 or 11-18 years), and others a narrower one (e.g. 7-11 or 16-19 years). Some draw few, if any, pupils from the ethnic minority communities, while others are populated almost entirely by such pupils. Despite all these differences, however, I believe we can identify some broad common features.

105

The desire to provide an education which is relevant to the world in which pupils live has meant that schools are concerned, for example, with the following objectives: to improve every pupil's knowledge and skills in mathematics and English; to provide experience of calculators and computers; to help children to understand (at least to some extent) some of the different cultures and religions present in our society; to improve the examination system, and to develop social and life skills.

The aims of the educational process have been variously stated. For example:

'Training of the pupil first as a person with a body, a mind and a spirit.'[3]

'To help each individual to realize the full powers in his personality.'[4]

'To help pupils understand the world in which they live.'[5]

'There is wide agreement about the purpose of learning at school, in particular that pupils should develop lively, enquiring minds, acquire understanding, knowledge and skills relevant to adult life and employment, and develop personal moral values.'[6]

These features and aims seem sensible enough. However, if we begin to probe beneath the surface, I believe we shall find aspects which should rightly concern Christians. Some of these, I hope, will emerge as we proceed.

APPLYING CHRISTIAN PRINCIPLES TO EDUCATION

Firstly, *why is it necessary to apply Christian principles to education?* The more broad and vague one's definitions are, the more agreement one can find. Conversely, the more specific our description is of the nature of education, the fewer will be the people who accept it. Yet even general descriptions sometimes beg basic questions. For example, in response to the second quotation above, one must ask, What are the 'full powers' of anyone's personality? Similarly, in response to the third, the question arises, How should the world be understood? Should we have a *Marxist* analysis, a *Christian* analysis, an *atheist* analysis, a *humanist* analysis, a *Hindu* analysis, etc.? Though some of these overlap with each other, there are also important differences between them. Perhaps the widely known phrase of R. S. Peters — 'to initiate children into worthwhile activities' — illustrates this best, as it leaves unanswered such important questions as, What is worth while? how do we measure? and who decides what counts as worth while?

Secondly, *why is it possible to apply Christian principles to education?* It will help us to see why this relationship can be developed if we look at the subject from different perspectives.

A theological perspective

A Christian view of the universe is that the whole of it is created by God. It is all His; He is concerned for it all, and it all relates together. We can make distinctions between various aspects of the world, but we cannot altogether separate them.

Not only is God the Creator; He is also omniscient and sovereign over the whole universe; He has total knowledge and control. Paul at Athens quoted a Greek poet who said, 'In him we live, and move, and have our being' (Acts 17:28). Paul wrote, 'In him [Christ] all things hold together' (Col. 1:17). Christ is the *uniting* force; we live in a '*uni*verse'. This unified view is not a collection of 'autonomous' disciplines or areas of thought. Hence, far from attempting to separate Christian theology and education, I hold that in principle it is possible to relate them. To establish a relationship between (true) knowledge in one area and (true) knowledge in another area will never result in contradiction. If there is an apparent contradiction between these areas, it means that one's apparent knowledge is defective at some point (or indeed at several points), or else that one has incorrectly related the two. For example, because Christians believe in one God, and that Christ is 'the image of the invisible God' (Col. 1:15), it is no contradiction to speak of both God and Christ in connection with creation, omniscience and sovereignty.

The assertion that it is possible to relate Christian principles to education because God has created a *uni*verse, not a collection of unrelated areas of life, means that Christians should not think and believe one thing in church, and adopt contradictory views on the same matters in other areas of their activity. It also means that teachers of integrity will not expect their pupils to shed their personal beliefs and values when they enter the classroom, and to pursue their studies as humanists, for example, if in fact that is not what they are.

An educational perspective

From an educational perspective much could be said, and here I can only develop one line of thinking. Peters has written that to be an educated person, one has to have a 'cognitive perspective'. By this he means that one must see each area in connection with other areas, understanding 'its place in a coherent pattern of life'. To

107

beaver away at one area, he says, not realizing its relationship with other areas, is to pursue 'an activity which is cognitively adrift'.[7] Or, to adopt Paul Hirst's phraseology, one can say that we must help pupils to understand the complex interrelations between the various forms of knowledge. Hirst believes that while each form has distinctive concepts and logical structure etc., these forms are not totally separate and unrelated to each other.[8] In response to this, I submit that Christians should say that it is possible for Christian beliefs to give a view of the world that can have an overarching function when it comes to relating different areas or forms of knowledge in a coherent pattern and making sense of the whole. This is what some would call having a cosmology or a metaphysic.

Hence, from an educational perspective it is vital to develop an overview and to see the world as a whole. Christianity does give such an overall view. There are various alternative world views available for children to adopt, and it is important to realize that they *are* developing some overall view of the world, even though it may be relatively subconscious or undeveloped. This is why education should not assume that a humanist or liberal theological outlook is superior to other views. To reject a Christian world view is not to become splendidly neutral, but to adopt some other non-Christian world view. At the level of relating the parts to the whole, every teacher and pupil has a world view which is affecting their personal view of education. In this sense, relating Christianity to education is certainly possible.

Sadly, some educationists, for all their professed intentions to examine everything critically, fail to appreciate that their basic view of the world should be examined in a fair and balanced way and not assumed to be true. Failure to pursue this task with pupils can amount to a kind of indoctrination.

The perspective of values

A third focus which demonstrates that it is possible to relate Christianity to education derives from the question of values. General statements about the aims of education may not be explicit about values, but when we start to unpack these general aims, value questions soon emerge.

If education were a value-free concept, it might not matter much whether Christianity were related to it or not. However, since education does involve values, it is relevant to examine the beliefs and values upheld by Christianity, and to consider whether or not education in Britain today generally demonstrates and commends the same values.

As we have seen, education involves views on what is *worth while* in life, on what the *purpose* of life is, on the *potential* of individuals, and on what our overall *view of the world* ought to be. These are value matters. Some people may not want their underlying values exposed, but one of the tasks of the Christian who is concerned about education is to make explicit the values at stake.

CHRISTIAN BELIEFS AND THEIR IMPLICATIONS

Having outlined these general principles, we shall go on to consider *what* it is that Christians should seek, and *how* they should seek it, by looking at the following examples of Christian beliefs and their implications for education.[9]

1. *Christian belief.* All people (including children) are created by God in His image (Gen. 1:26f.; 9:6; James 3:9).

Implication for education. Every child matters; every child has inherent worth, regardless of their abilities academically, musically or in any other way. Therefore we are to value every child highly, even those whose potential for academic achievement seems very limited. Being highly literate themselves, teachers perhaps find it easy to despise, or at least have little time for, those who find reading and writing hard. One teacher I know frequently refers to such children as 'the rubbish'. Christians may not use that description, but we are not necessarily immune from the same attitude. Perhaps the school curriculum is sometimes too much geared to the highly literate pupils and too much examination-orientated. If we felt more deeply that every child matters, we might not rest so content with a system that gives many children an irrelevant curriculum, and we might welcome more enthusiastically attempts to develop new and more appropriate courses.

2. *Christian belief.* Though made in God's image, everyone is 'fallen' and has a bias towards evil as well as a potential for good. This potential for good has to be developed, and the bias towards evil has to be restrained (Gen. 3; Rom. 3:9-18,22f.; Phil. 4:8).

Implication for education. Moral education is a vital part of education. This means that when children act rightly, such behaviour should be praised and encouraged (1 Pet. 2:14). It also implies that some sanctions or external discipline must continue to be available (Eph. 6:1-4; Heb. 12:7-11). Furthermore, we must help children to

109

recognize the moral choices and temptations to evil with which they are faced, and assist them in developing their own self-discipline.

3. *Christian belief*. Parents have some responsibility for the upbringing of their children (Deut. 6:6f.; Eph. 6:4). In current terminology we would say that they have particular responsibilities in the areas of moral and religious/spiritual education.

Implication for education. Children should be taught in ways that wise and careful parents can accept, and there must be respect for the parents' legitimate interest in the school process, specifically in *what* is taught and *how*. This means keeping parents informed about the curriculum and, in outline terms, the syllabuses too. It also means giving the parents adequate time for confidential consultations. Some so-called Parents' Evenings are like hectic and disorganized cattle markets. If the implication of the first Christian belief quoted was that every child matters, the implication of this teaching is that every parent matters.[10]

4. *Christian belief*. There is more to life than gaining status and material wealth. Jesus said, 'Take heed, and beware of all covetousness; for a man's life does not consist in the abundance of his possessions' (Luke 12:15). He also said:

> You know that the rulers of the Gentiles lord it over them, and their great men exercise authority over them. It shall not be so among you; but whoever would be great among you must be your servant, and whoever would be first among you must be your slave; even as the Son of man came not to be served but to serve, and to give his life as a ransom for many.   Matthew 20:25-28

Implication for education. We must help children, by personal example and words of encouragement, not to be selfish and not to seek merely for pleasure and power. Some teachers have openly declared, or given children the clear impression, that they must behave and work hard or else they will not get a good job, by which they mean position and pay. Preparation for the world of work and the world of leisure is important, of course, but we ought not to teach children, directly or indirectly, that the major purpose of life is to obtain high status and high pay. It is the testimony of both Old and New Testaments that the first consideration is to love God 'with all your heart and with all your soul and with all your mind', and to 'love your neighbour as yourself' (Matt. 22:37,39; cf. Deut. 6:5; Lev. 19:18). According to the Christian ideal of service, what one can give is more important than what one can get, and this ideal should be commended to all children.

I can well understand the Christian assessment that the standard set is impossible for pupils to achieve, especially while they are not Christians, and I agree with this. Nevertheless I feel, firstly, that if pupils are to begin to understand Christianity they must learn to appreciate at least something of what the life of discipleship involves, and, secondly, that our Lord taught principles of moderation, generosity, humility and service which are worth commending to all children (though of course without any assumption that salvation by works is possible).

WORKING OUT THE PRINCIPLES IN PRACTICE

Responsibilities for applying Christian truths to education lie with individuals (Christian parents and other Christians) and with local churches as bodies of believers. I suggest we start by considering how Christian parents can fulfil their responsibilities in this area.

The role of Christian parents

For those who are Christian parents the beliefs mentioned above point to obvious responsibilities. So much depends on our attitudes to our children. We should not be so ambitious for them that they feel they cannot match our expectations. Clearly they do have responsibilities to develop their talents, but we should seek to assure them that God loves them deeply and values them highly, irrespective of their achievements or failures at school, and so do we. The ultimate indication of God's valuation of us is Christ's death on our behalf; it is not in any way conditional upon our attainments, academic or otherwise.

In terms of customs and habits which are cultural, or which vary quite properly from family to family, there are no absolute rules. But there are some definite standards set out in Scripture, and these are not variable according to culture or family preferences. Telling the truth, honouring parents and not stealing are obvious examples. In such matters there will be occasions when parents should show their recognition of the fact that a child has kept to the standard when it was not easy to do so. There will also be occasions when parents should, with explanation, exercise some external discipline, involving punishment which is appropriate but never vindictive (easier to say than to do!).

Parental responsibility for children's upbringing and education includes various minimum obligations: for example, reading carefully the books and letters they bring home, and attending the school for discussion with teachers. There are other obligations, however, on which I want to say a little more.

Parental responsibility includes prayer

It is one thing to say that this is obvious, but perhaps quite another thing to pray personally for the following: the heads, teachers and governors of our children's schools (individually, by name); members of the Local Education Authority's Education Committee; the pupils in the schools (children of Christian parents and others); the Religious Education lessons and school assemblies; Christian young people training to be teachers or considering embarking on such training, and so on. In a number of places, Christian parents with children at a particular school meet together to pray for that school. Clearly this may involve Christians from several churches.

Parental responsibility includes teaching

We should not leave the teaching of our children entirely to others, either those at school or those at church. Parents themselves have much to teach their children. As parents we have a particular part to play in teaching them the truths of Scripture. There are benefits in having a regular time for this, but we need to keep the methods and timing under review. We shall also want opportunities, of course, to share with our children what God has done and is still doing for us and in us, and to pray together as a family. If the parents' faith is real enough to influence every part of their life, the exhortation to talk of God's commandments 'when you sit in your house, and when you walk by the way . . .' (Deut. 6:7) will be readily heeded. That will be more effective than a religious practice which is confined to a couple of minutes at breakfast and a couple of hours on Sundays.

To go further, I believe that Christian parents have a teaching role in every subject, not just in religion. The events of daily life, both routine and special, workdays and holidays, present many teaching opportunities, and we should look out for these. Often Christian parents have better opportunities to explain a Christian perspective than anyone else.

Parental responsibility includes listening

There is no substitute for spending time with one's children. It is only as we maintain a deep relationship of mutual trust that our

112

children will share with us what their school life is like. It is essential that we know what they are being taught; without this we cannot possibly feed in correctives when necessary. It requires skill to listen carefully and draw out information without making children feel they are being interrogated.

Christians who are not parents, or those whose children have not started school or have left school, can take on board some of these responsibilities. They can pray for the local schools, including the Christians involved in them. Some of them, whether parents or not, may be called by God to become more involved than most. Taking up a career in teaching is one possible way — there are particular shortages of teachers in some fields — but it is by no means the only one. Other ways of getting involved include, for example, hearing children read, observation at the swimming pool, providing transport for sports matches, membership of the school's governing body, participation in a Parents' Association or Parent-Teacher Association, donating Christian books to the school or writing letters of thanks for something good in the school. Ministers and pastors may sometimes be invited to lead assemblies, but there is no reason why we should think only in terms of this kind of link. Precisely what one is able to do or say in terms of a contribution from a Christian perspective is likely to vary from one situation to another, but the more one considers the implications of Christian beliefs for education, the more one is alert to, and prepared for, the needs and opportunities for influence.

It is important that those who are called to particular avenues of service should seek to make a *positive* contribution. Christian beliefs yield enough positive insights for Christians to have much to say of a positive nature when the time is right. Positive suggestions, if politely made, help establish good relationships, which in turn provide a trusting context for a disapproving comment, should this at some time be necessary. We should also not underestimate the value of asking pointed questions. Sometimes a few timely and pertinent questions can be used to expose the inadequacy of a practice or proposal.

The role of the churches

One part which the churches can play is to remind parents from time to time of their responsibilities. They can also give regular support and encouragement to Christian parents and any others who seek to be involved in some way in education.

Christians who get more involved in education than most, seeking to be effective as 'salt' in that sphere, can easily feel isolated.

Some of those with whom they have contact can be suspicious and dismissive, and it is only to be expected that opposition from non-Christians will occur from time to time. Lack of interest from fellow Christians, especially those within one's own church, is tantamount to opposition and is harder to bear. It can be a lonely path to tread, and the support of a few sympathetic Christian friends, at a level deeper than is possible by the church as a whole, can be a vital ingredient to help them persevere with the task at hand.

The churches can certainly give a lead in ensuring that their prayer life is broad enough to encompass the local schools and colleges. Some who are in touch with the situation can often bring news of Christian teachers, Christian pupils, the Christian Union or some activity or need in the school, without breaking any confidences. Some churches earmark one Sunday a year when particular attention is given to some aspects of Christianity and education.

I believe that, in the normal run of things, attempts to influence the schools are best made by individuals in their own name rather than by the church as a whole or by someone on behalf of the church. The church exists primarily to worship God, to build up the saints and to proclaim the gospel.

However, I would not wish to be adamant and say that nothing should ever be done in the name of the church. On some matters, I know, it may be unlikely that sufficient agreement can be reached (about the use of corporal punishment in school, for example). Nevertheless, on some occasions an issue could arise on which there was unanimous, or nearly unanimous, agreement. That could happen, for instance, if a school were to mount an education course which strongly commended sexual intercourse outside marriage and loudly ridiculed chastity, or a course on the occult that expected pupils to participate in occult activities. Supposing that all avenues commensurate with Christian behaviour had been explored at length by individuals without securing any agreement on the school's part to change its stance, I can find no biblical reason why the church as a body of believers should remain silent indefinitely on such matters. Complex questions would arise such as, Precisely what should be said? and when, by whom, and to whom? But these may not be insurmountable. While it is true that such action could distract the church from her main role, it could also be a natural, proper expression and outworking of its compassion and concern for the welfare of local children, those who are in some way connected with the church and those who are not. *I want to stress, however, that I see this sort of action as the exception rather than the rule.*

114

CHRIST AND THE GOSPEL

It would be possible to argue that biblical teaching about the nature of human beings, about parenthood and about human relationships is the only biblical material we can apply to education. It is not surprising that the application of Christian truths to education should so often start with the doctrine of man, for school education is principally concerned with people, especially children, and their nature is so obvious a starting-point. However, Christians should be severely dissatisfied with this limited, though important, application. Why? Because it leaves out Christ and the gospel.

We should not only consider man made in the image of God, valuable, fallen, spoilt, crippled, imprisoned, etc., for we have other 'models' of man, if that is not an irreverent way of putting it. There is Christ, the Son of Man, who is 'the image of the invisible God' (Col. 1:15). However, that is not all there is to say. If we see Christ merely as an example towering above us, leaving us struggling to reach an impossibly high standard with grossly insufficient will-power, it is desperately depressing. But, thankfully, we have not been abandoned to this soul-destroying task. By His life, death and resurrection Jesus made possible a redeemed man. This is salvation 'by grace . . . through faith' (Eph. 2:8), a way of salvation totally different from the futile treadmill of salvation by works.

If we are involved in any discussion about 'individual potential' or 'understanding life', this is one point at which a distinctively Christian view emerges. At times, some people who are not Christians accept something of the Christian view of man, regarding him as a fine being, but flawed. Outside Christianity, however, it is not seriously believed that in Christ alone a lost fallen man can become a *redeemed* fallen man.

Christians are not always in a position to explain the height to which God can raise man. Sometimes we sense that the time is not right; sometimes we are conscious of lack of interest or hostility, and we hesitate to 'cast pearls before swine' (Matt. 7:6). And sometimes the time is right and the opportunity is there, but we lack the courage. Whatever the explanation, when the biblical view of human potential and destiny is overlooked, Christians must regret it. This potential and destiny is, of course, very far-reaching: it encompasses the resurrection of the body (1 Cor. 15) and 'an inheritance which is imperishable, undefiled and unfading, kept in heaven . . .' (1 Pet. 1:4).

Our present society, by and large, is happy for children to evaluate critically such beliefs from a non-Christian stance, and it

115

often looks with scorn upon children who accept them. That is one reason why some Christians support alternatives, and I want to comment briefly on this in the final section of this chapter.

CHRISTIAN SCHOOLS

It ought not to be surprising if Christians whose children attend church schools want those schools to be recognizably Christian. What that means is open to debate, and some church schools have a tradition of a hundred years or more from which to learn. While many church schools are 'aided' or 'controlled' by their local education authorities, some are independent. Whatever the school's status, a vigorous reconsideration of the implications of having a Christian foundation would be worth while. This means more than talking in general terms about ethos. We need to ask whether commitment to Christian beliefs and principles has implications for the curriculum, the content of schemes of work and lessons, teaching styles, staff appointments, means of assessment, relations with parents, etc.

A number of new Christian schools have been opened in the last 20 years. Some use 'programmed learning' materials produced by Accelerated Christian Education in the United States: some do not. Some are linked with the Christian Parent-Teacher League: some are not. (This is not the place to assess the suitability of the ACE materials or the various possible ways of governing such schools.)

It appears to me that there is no clear biblical reason for saying either that God requires parents to send their children to separate Christian schools or that the establishment of such schools is forbidden or is an unchristian thing to do. Hence we can neither say that it is obligatory for Christians to set up and support such schools nor that it is wrong to do so. What we can say, however, is that it can be valuable to take up opportunities for exploring various options for educating children. As there is no single, perfect style of education, it is likely that the churches can learn much from the experience of seeking to apply Christian principles in various kinds of schools. That is not to say that *any* experiment is valid, or that children may be used as fodder for research. It is simply to acknowledge that in the present climate of opinion in Britain it is often extremely difficult for an ordinary maintained school to commend Christian values and beliefs. Attempts to do so are easily dubbed evangelistic, confessional or indoctrinatory.

On the other hand, independent Christian schools have more freedom to allow Christian values and beliefs to influence and permeate every area of the school's life. A school must endeavour to ensure that this happens in practice if it is to be truthfully described as a Christian school. Words alone are not enough, whether in the school's name, motto, prospectus, trust deed, constitution or elsewhere. Setting up and running a Christian school is a complex business, not to be embarked upon in haste.

Local churches and groups of Christians which support a Christian school can continue to show concern and give support for the other schools in their locality. It is possible for their Christian concern and compassion to be as wide as this. Indeed, if they are not to betray their responsibility to act as salt in society, this broader concern is essential; it is a poor thing if the attitude is one of letting the other schools rot. Pride, self-satisfaction and indifference are not Christian virtues, and that applies whether or not we welcome the emergence of new Christian schools.

NOTES

1 I realize that education does not come only through schools (e.g. homes and clubs also have influence), but for the sake of convenience I take that as read and assume that the schools play a large part in the educational process.

I commented briefly on the effect of humanism on our society and our schools in *Whose Child?* (Association of Christian Teachers of Wales, 1982, pp.1-3), and I do not repeat those comments here, though they are relevant to an understanding of the background to the nature of contemporary British schools.

2 These figures are given in *Social Trends* 18, 1988 Edition, Table 3.3 (HMSO, 1988).

3 The Spens Report, *Secondary Education* (HMSO, 1938), p.145.

4 The Norwood Report, *Curriculum and Examinations in Secondary Schools* (HMSO, 1943), p.viii.

5 *The School Curriculum* (Department of Education and Science, 1981).

6 *Better Schools — A Summary* (Department of Education and Science, 1985), p.4.

7 R. S. Peters, *Ethics and Education* (George, Allen & Unwin, 1970), p.31.

8 P. H. Hirst, *Knowledge and the Curriculum* (Routledge & Kegan Paul, 1974), pp.47,52.

9 Several other examples are given in my article 'The Aims of Education' in *Spectrum* 15.3 (Summer 1983), pp.7-11.

10 The Association of Christian Teachers of Wales has produced a most helpful leaflet on this theme entitled *A Call to Christian Parents*, available from the address below.

QUESTIONS FOR DISCUSSION

a) Does being a Christian, or not being a Christian, make any difference to my view of education? Could it and should it make a difference? If so, what are some of the differences?

b) How does the present state of education in Britain relate to what ideally Christians would like the situation to be?

c) Who is responsible for the education of children (e.g. churches, governments, parents, pupils)? What material in Scripture is relevant to this matter?

d) What support do I and the church of which I am a member give to education? What support would Christian governors, pupils, parents and teachers appreciate? How could we be more involved in local schools and colleges?

FURTHER READING

B. V. Hill, *Faith at the Blackboard* (Eerdmans, 1982, distributed in the UK by Paternoster Press)

F. Hughes, *Whose Child?* (Association of Christian Teachers of Wales, 1982)

C. Martin, *You've Got to Start Somewhere When You Think About Education* (Inter-Varsity Press, 1979)

C. Martin, *Have Schools Lost Their Way?* (Grove Books, 1980)

P. May, *Which Way to School?* (Lion Publishing, 1972)

P. May, *Which Way to Teach?* (Inter-Varsity Press, 1981)

M. L. Peterson, *Philosophy of Education: Issues and Options* (Inter-Varsity Press, 1987)

While aimed mainly at Christians working in the field of education, *Spectrum,* the magazine of the Association of Christian Teachers, is of wider interest. It is published twice a year on behalf of ACT by the Paternoster Press. The addresses of the Association of Christian Teachers are given below:

ACT, 2 Romeland Hill, St Albans, Hertfordshire AL3 4ET.
ACT Wales, 38 Darren View, Crickhowell, Powys NP8 1DS.
ACT Scotland, 38 Ardconnel Street, Inverness.

8

The Role of Women in the Local Church

ELIZABETH CATHERWOOD

Of all the subjects which are covered in this book, it seems to me
that this one, concerning the role of women in the local church, is
the thorniest and the one most beset by pitfalls of every kind. Indeed, the whole question of the role of women in general is one that
is currently vexing and arousing women in every society. Women
right across the spectrum, from the ardent — even anarchic — sup-
porter of the Women's Liberation Movement to the elderly 'conservative' lady, are being forced to reconsider their position, and to
see how they fit into the society in which they find themselves.
Various, and frequently violent, are the views expressed on both
sides, and in the middle of all this the Christian woman is to be
found battling her way through the problems. Her perplexity is, of
course, compounded by the fact that she not only faces the common problems of her sisters in society — career versus
motherhood, for example — but she also has to think through,
honestly and biblically, how in the face of all the pressures round
her she should be fulfilling her God-given role in His family, the
church.

She can find many books which try to help her, but the trouble is
that on so many points the experts, including the evangelical ones,
hold diametrically opposite opinions. It was not for nothing that
the role of women was included in a series of evangelical books aptly named *When Christians Disagree!* Conferences deal with the
problems and speakers speak on them, while Christian groups are
increasingly setting up gladiatorial debates, with the known ex-
ponents of different views sitting opposite each other in true BBC
confrontational style. The Christian woman can almost feel
bludgeoned by the amount of argument going on around her and at
her. 'Why', wailed an American student to me, 'wasn't I born a
man? It would have been so much simpler!'

119

Given the world in which we are living, all this is inevitable to a certain extent. Yet the sad thing is that the controversial areas completely swamp our concentration on the positive aspects of all that we women should be doing for the Lord in His church. So it is my hope that by the end of this particular venture into the battle we shall be thanking God for the responsibilities, possibilities and opportunities open to women to glorify Him and to work for Him.

CULTURE, TRADITION OR SCRIPTURE?

There are certain general principles that we need to lay down before we look at the different aspects of the subject in detail. First, we need to keep a balance between being swayed by past tradition on the one hand, and the modern spirit of the age on the other. Neither of these approaches is biblical, though both may contain elements that are scripturally right. We are so easily influenced by our culture, by what 'has always been done', often giving culture an almost theological allegiance.

A practical illustration of this happened at an inter-chapel gathering some time ago. Following the afternoon meeting, tea was provided by the ladies of the host church. An abundance of food was provided, everyone ate well, there were a few votes of thanks to the host church, and then one of the ministers rose to his feet and said quite seriously, 'The ladies will now exercise their Christian ministry and do the washing up.' Now was that Pauline teaching or was it traditionalism — or even chauvinism? What about honouring women as 'weaker partners', or men 'cherishing' the wives that God had given them? And is washing the dishes demeaning to men who claim to follow the Master who washed His disciples' feet? All too often in our churches women are expected to be Marthas and are too occupied, or too tired, to become the Marys that many of them long to be.

But it is not only the men who are at fault. Frequently in this debate I have found the stiffest opposition to change coming from the older women. They do have, of course, a real function in dealing with their younger sisters, and I shall deal with this later. Yet if the point is made that women should be given greater freedom to participate in the church, or that men should be more caring, the response from women who are over fifty may well be, 'It wasn't easy in *our* day, but *we* managed, so why can't they?' Nothing is more exasperating to the younger generation, and justifiably so. The fact that something has always been done — or endured — does not make it right or biblical.

120

There is no doubt that much of the stridency on the women's scene is due to the oppressive treatment of women in the past. This is true of society in general, and the church too is not without guilt. Yet though we may rightly feel strongly about, and condemn, past injustice, we should not allow ourselves to go to the opposite extreme and be taken over by the spirit of the age. One of the main planks of the Women's Liberation Movement, in reaction to the past, is that women should be free to express themselves in whatever way they choose. A strong feminist would feel that a woman can choose to have her baby aborted; husband, children and everyone else must fit into her career plans, and some have even left their children in an attempt to 'find themselves'.[1] Now let us be clear about this. It is certainly true that over the centuries women have been deprived of many 'inalienable rights', and still are deprived of them in some countries. We need to be grateful to those, both Christian and otherwise, who have campaigned to give us more liberty. But is strident self-assertion really a Christian virtue? 'Why can't I preach to men *if I want to?*' asked a confident young woman at a Christian conference — and there are many like her. But what about duties, responsibilities and Christian obedience, as well as rights?

Furthermore, some of the second generation of feminist writers are beginning to query the assertions of the first. They realize that losses may have been linked in with the gains, and they are emphasizing the need to be women as well as free. It is sad to observe that as the world realizes that perhaps it has made mistakes, the Christian church, ten years out of date, feels it must give women new rights in order to keep up with the Ms Jones of the early seventies!

Sadly, to return to the other extreme again, there is also a spirit at large in the Western world at the moment which can only be described as an evangelical backlash. Fear of increasing female emancipation has led many men — 'conservative fellows of the fundamentalist sort' — to make certain that *their* women are kept in their place. Biblical verses are wrenched from their context, married women are allowed to possess nothing of their own (that was preached not long ago from an evangelical pulpit!), and total obedience is demanded from the women in the church. Such overreaction can only do immense harm to the cause of the gospel and bring unnecessary suffering to the women concerned, quite apart from the seriousness of mishandling the Word of God.

In the light of all these extremes, those of us who are Christians need to keep our heads and to be sure that we are not 'tossed back and forth by the waves, and blown here and there by every wind of teaching' (Eph. 4:14). We need to 'prove all things' and to be sure of our spirit and motives before we speak or act. We need to remember always Paul's injunction: 'Do not conform any longer to the pattern of this world, but be transformed by the renewing of your mind' (Rom. 12:2). We need the 'self-discipline' of which Paul speaks to Timothy (2 Tim. 1:7). The Authorized Version translates this word as 'a sound mind', which conveys the same basic idea. Much heat is often generated in discussion on this subject, but for us it should be true that 'speaking the truth in love, we will in all things [the role of women included] grow up into him who is the Head, that is, Christ' (Eph. 4:15).

MALE AND FEMALE DIFFERENCES?

The second general principle we need to keep in mind is that we must beware of making sweeping generalizations about male/female qualities when we discuss the role of women in the church. Common examples of this are that women are more sensitive, men are more logical; women have greater patience, men are less bothered by detail . . . and so on. The trouble with all such statements as a basis for church government and policy is that they lead to endless arguments as to their veracity. Immediately examples are cited of impatient, tactless women and muddle-headed, fussy men, and others then try to say that such people are exceptions. But all this, it seems to me, is unhelpful and most frustrating to women. There are very few places in the Bible where these specific distinctions are drawn. Reference is made to the strength of men — 'Quit you like men, be strong' (1 Cor. 16:13 AV) — and to the weakness of women (1 Pet. 3:7), but these may well refer to differences in our physical make-up. Then the commentators are divided as to whether Paul's reference to the first woman being deceived (1 Tim. 2:14) carries in it the implication that this was because of her feminine nature, or whether it is simply an allusion to the historical fact of what happened in the Garden of Eden. Again, the gentle, submissive spirit which Peter encourages wives to cultivate (1 Pet. 3:1) he also asks of those being persecuted (1 Pet. 3:14-16; cf. Eph. 5:21).

Why do I emphasize these points? It is because many strong, articulate, energetic women are frequently depressed by being told that they are *unbiblically* unfeminine. Or they are told that they may not teach, because men have clearer minds and are therefore more suitable for proclaiming the truth. People seem to forget Deborah and the woman of Proverbs 31, not to speak of Priscilla!

No, all such argument is unhelpful, because whatever our individual characters may be, the Bible uses precept and example to lay down guidelines about woman's God-given role and behaviour — in her family, in society and in the church. In the end this is the Christian woman's assurance and security, and the only basis on which she can be helped by her brothers in Christ.

THE BIBLE'S GENERAL PRINCIPLES

My third principle would be that when considering the biblical teaching about woman's role, we should carefully adhere to the Bible's general principles. Modern expositors become very excited about the exact connotation of a particular word — *authentein* ('to have authority') in 1 Timothy 2:12, for example. They build up radical ideas from it and argue about its sources and usage. Learned papers are written about the various nuances, different conclusions are reached, and the average Christian woman is left feeling that she needs a doctorate in theology before she knows how to behave. Perhaps we need to remind ourselves of Paul's words to Timothy: 'Warn them before God against quarrelling about words; it is of no value and only ruins those who listen. Do your best to present yourself to God as one approved, a workman who does not need to be ashamed and who correctly handles the word of truth!' (2 Tim. 2:14-15).

WOMEN AND PREACHING

So then, with all these provisos in mind, let us move on to consider what part women have to play in the local church. Perhaps the best thing to do is to plunge in at the deep end and say that, as I understand Scripture, our role does not include that of pastor, elder, or public teacher where men are present. Woman, in Paul's words, is not 'to have authority over a man'. This is a quotation, of course, from that controversial passage, 1 Timothy 2:11-15, and it is here that the reason for my third general guideline becomes apparent. Both sides of the 'woman-in-leadership' divide base their argument on their understanding of the words in this chapter and in the other relevant passages in 1 Corinthians 11 and 14. It seems to me, however, that from beginning to end the Bible shows that, in the plan of God for His people, headship (i.e. authority) rests upon the man.

We now need to consider the main arguments advanced by those who would support the ordination of women and the role of women as public teachers *where men are present*. This last phrase is important, because it seems quite clear from passages like Titus 2:4 that a teaching ministry to other women is encouraged. Furthermore, the role of women in teaching children is implicit in verses like 1 Timothy 5:10, since in the Bible the bringing up of children always seems to include the duty of leading them in the ways of the Lord. Then, of course, the example of Priscilla shows that privately a woman can be of great value in making clear the truth to a man who has not understood it.

Those who adopt a 'radical' view of women in church leadership put forward a number of arguments. In outline they are:

1. Woman was indeed made subject to man by the Fall. But now the cross of Christ has done away with all that, and she is restored to full equality with man in all things, as was intended at the creation.

2. Paul lists many women who laboured with him in the Lord. Can we imagine that they, and others like them — Lydia, for example — never taught?

3. *Authentein* (the Greek word translated 'to have authority' in 1 Timothy 2:12) does not mean that women cannot teach or be in authority. It means either (a) that wives may not teach or officiously try to put their husbands right, or (b) that, when teaching or leading, women must not do this in a domineering manner.

4. In these passages we must never forget the context. The women in Ephesus and Corinth were uncontrolled chatterers, poorly educated, and upsetting the social mores of their day by their abuse of Christian freedom. Therefore, what is said to them clearly cannot be applied to the well-educated women of our emancipated society.

5. We must remember that Paul, the ex-rabbi, was writing within his own cultural outlook. As we can see from his teaching in Galatians 3:28, the apostle Paul saw clearly that men and women were equal. But his rabbinical upbringing died hard, and he was anxious not to upset contemporary society. So his teaching on this point has little to do with the church of today.

It is impossible to give a comprehensive answer to these wide-ranging arguments in the brief space available, but the biblical position, as I understand it, is this. Men and women are equal in creation (Gen. 1:27), salvation (Gal. 3:28), in all the blessings of the Christian life and in the certainty of glory. From the beginning, too, women have played an important part in the life of God's people, often against the background of a pagan society where women were discounted and despised. Ruth, Rahab, Deborah, Abigail, Huldah, Manoah's wife, the Shunammite woman, Miriam and Jochebed all had an understanding of the ways of God; they acted as women of faith and showed a deep loyalty and devotion to God's plan for Israel. The Lord Jesus had around Him women who dedicated themselves to His service and whom He loved. There were clearly women in the upper room on the day of Pentecost (cf. Acts 1:14), and we read of many in the book of Acts (e.g. 9:36; 12:12; 16:14; 18:2ff.). Furthermore, we would agree that Paul respected and appreciated the women who worked with him, though the second argument quoted above, it seems to me, is an argument from silence, which is always unsatisfactory, and in this case flies in the face of 1 Timothy 2.

While all this underlines the fact that women are by no means second-class citizens in the kingdom of God, it in no way militates against the equally biblical truth that they have been given a different role. 'The Bible sees nothing incompatible in headship and equality.'[2]

'It is not good for man to be alone', God said at the beginning; 'I will make a helper suitable for him' (Gen. 2:18). Paul refers to this when he tells the Corinthians: 'For man did not come from woman, but woman from man; neither was man created for woman, but woman for man' (1 Cor. 11:8-9). The word 'for' is used to introduce his explanation of a statement he made at the beginning of his argument: 'Now I want you to realise that the head of every man is Christ, and the head of the woman is man, and the head of Christ is God' (v.3). Therefore, in marriage (cf. Eph. 5, Col. 4, Titus 2, 1 Pet. 3) and in the organization of the church it is the man who is to lead. Deborah, often quoted as the Old Testament feminist, saw this clearly. 'Very well . . . I will go with you [into battle if you insist]', she says to the feeble Barak. 'But because of the way you are going about this, the honour will not be yours, for the Lord will hand Sisera over to a woman' (Judg. 4:9). The divine order of leadership is clearly demonstrated throughout the Old Testament. As John Stott has said, 'This is not chauvinism but creationism.'[3]

The New Testament nowhere suggests that this *order* has been abrogated by the cross; but our *behaviour* as men and women within our different roles is something which should be transformed by the love of God poured into our hearts by the Holy Spirit. The men lead, but neither ruthlessly nor unlovingly: the women submit to their leadership as to Christ, whose head is God and who said, 'I seek not my own will but the will of him who sent me' (John 5:30 RSV).

Paul also takes the argument for the authority of the man one stage further. In 1 Timothy 2:12-14 he speaks strongly: 'I do not permit . . .', he says, and then he gives his reasons. First, because 'Adam was formed first, then Eve', and then he goes on, 'And Adam was not the one deceived; it was the woman who was deceived and became a sinner.' There, in the Garden of Eden, Eve stepped out of her appointed role and so led Adam into sin. R. C. H. Lenski puts it well in his commentary on this passage: 'Both Eve and Adam had to violate not only the command of God not to eat, but also their respective positions towards each other, in order to effect the Fall . . . Eve usurped the headship in the Fall; Adam, who was the head, became the feet and followed Eve in the *parabasis* (the "stepping aside").'

This to me is always the authoritative answer to the contextual or cultural objection. Paul is not dealing here merely with the problem of *Ephesian* women. And if this is an ex-rabbinical 'hang-up', how can we be sure that many other passages — some of them more crucial to our faith than this one — are not a similar legacy from Paul's days as a rabbi? We cannot accept or reject passages of Scripture at will like this. No, Paul is here dealing with the human problem of running the church. It is true that he sets it in a context, but the context is that of the history of mankind and of God's saving purpose for His people. His concern in these passages is not only with Ephesian education or chattering Corinthians; he takes us back to creation, to the Fall, to the Trinity, and to the work of the Godhead in our salvation. Those are not just Paul's ideas for the first century, but the revealed Word of God, God's plan for the church in the world. And thank God for that!

THE MINISTRY OF WOMEN

It must be stressed, however, that submission nowhere means subjugation. A woman may not be a pastor or an elder (neither, incidentally, may most of the men in the church), but she is a vital member of the body of Christ. Furthermore, if a woman believes that God has given her the gift of teaching, and this is ratified by the church, there is ample scope for her to exercise this gift, both in the local congregation and outside it, in women's meetings of all kinds.

I sometimes feel a book could be written about the importance of those often despised 'Women's Meetings'. Sometimes they are gatherings where mainly elderly ladies come in for a chat and a cup of tea. Such women are often lonely, frightened and lost; they need

126

to know that they are loved, and to hear of One who can be their Saviour. Or again, at the opposite end of the spectrum, there can be lively Bible classes and meetings for women of all ages. Some may be older in years but may not have been converted for long; others may be young in years and, with their toddlers safely esconced in a crèche, may be glad to get out and have an opportunity to talk. But amongst these and other groups there may be a real hunger for the Word of God. We live in an unchurched and untaught age, when young people often have no Christian background at all. I remember once being at a flourishing meeting for young wives and referring to something which Paul had written to Timothy. A girl said at the end, 'I didn't know Paul wrote letters like that. It sounds great. What did you say the young man's name was?'

Such a ministry can be of considerable significance in a church's life. Let me illustrate this. A middle-aged woman, well-grounded in the Scriptures, had for some years run a weekly women's Bible study in her home. The members of the group had enjoyed and profited from this and began talking about what they had learned to other women in the church. It was a church which was growing steadily and seeing many conversions, but the teaching was not strong and there were many problems. Some of the leaders of the other women's groups in the church began to turn to her, and ultimately she was asked to oversee the programme for all such groups. Through her teaching gifts she passed on her knowledge to the other leaders, who in their turn learned to share it with their groups. The women began to talk to their husbands and to teach their children, and so the whole church was edified.

It is sad that many women, fearful of stepping outside their role, often feel that they do not need to bother to immerse themselves in scriptural truth. They are content to be devotional and to leave doctrine to the men. Priscilla clearly did not take that attitude, and we in our day are surrounded by men who in different ways resemble Apollos (cf. Acts 18:24-28). There are the hyper-Reformed ones who think that if they just quote chunks of the Puritans their congregations are bound to be edified; then there are hyper-active men who exhaust the people by one campaign or project after another, and hyper-emotional ones who think that by much singing and sharing, church members will learn doctrine by osmosis. All such men need help, and the woman who truly knows her God and has studied deeply in His Word can get alongside them and, like Priscilla, explain to them 'the way of God more adequately' (Acts 18:26). Priscilla did this with Aquila, I know, but there are many men in the ministry today who owe much to the faithful wisdom of the women in the church, both single and married.[4] Yet all this is to be done in the biblical context of submission, 'quietness', modesty and the total absence of a strident authoritarian attitude.

The question that frequently harasses women, anxious to be right when men are present, is to know exactly what 'teaching' is. 'The public teacher of God's people does not only tell others what they need to know, but in the capacity of a teacher he stands before his audience to rule and govern it with the Word.' That is R. C. H. Lenski's definition. It is helpful, and it precludes a popular point of view that it is fine for a woman to teach, provided an elder is taking the service or chairing the meeting. Teaching in itself is authoritative. But what about writing (or sharing in writing!) a book where Scripture is quoted and adduced? Men read it. Or what about broadcasting? Men hear it. These situations and many others are often difficult to assess, and Christian pastors and leaders need to be gentle and long-suffering with the women who try to work them out.[5] Such men need to encourage on the one hand, and yet to avoid leading women into unbiblical situations out of a fear of appearing chauvinistic.

Evangelism is another difficult area. God has often used women to bring many to Christ through public evangelism — Henrietta Soltau and 'the Marechal' Booth, for example. Is wooing people with the gospel different from 'ruling and governing' an audience 'with the Word'? I am not sure.

Again, we must avoid an over-legalistic attitude when we look at the mission field. Someone has said that this is a cop-out: 'Not OK at home — OK abroad!' But surely this is not so. In some areas of the world there are no men, neither nationals of the country nor expatriates, to engage in this teaching ministry. The overriding priority in such a situation is to make known God's truth. Yet this is not the biblical norm, and we should also not forget that Paul was speaking to exceedingly young missionary churches. A wise and mature woman worker with the former China Inland Mission once said to me, 'If more men came to the mission field, this problem wouldn't arise; and if a woman missionary stopped teaching publicly much sooner and quietly taught the man who, she believed, was God's chosen teacher for the new church, it would be better for the church, better for the man, and', she added with a twinkle in her eye, 'better for the woman missionary too!'

Praying and prophesying are clearly activities in the worshipping church that are open to women (1 Cor. 11:5), though here again there are many varying explanations of what 'prophesying' means. Some would confine it to a direct foretelling of the future for the church, while others feel that Paul is referring here to the possibility of a woman sharing with the church something which she herself has learned from the Word of God, or an understanding which she has received which is in accordance with His Word and is relevant to the church and its members.

Biblical teaching is not so specific when it comes to general speaking in the church, but it would not seem to preclude a woman, if she is asked, giving her opinion on some issue to the body of the church (e.g. a teacher speaking on education, or a doctor on euthanasia), or joining in a discussion as a member of the church. However, a preponderance of female voices brings with it the danger of an unbiblical imbalance, and Paul seems to say that for the married woman it is better if her husband takes the lead in church gatherings. I say 'seems' because there have been many different expositions of 1 Corinthians 14:33-36. Indeed I find these verses the most difficult to explain satisfactorily and conclusively. This is particularly true of verse 36: 'Did the word of God originate with you? Or are you the only people it has reached?' Yet if we abide by the principle of comparing scripture with scripture and holding on to the broad general teaching of the Bible, it seems to me that Paul cannot have meant absolute silence as a rule for the women of the church. However one may interpret the head-covering issue of 1 Corinthians 11, it is clear, as we have already seen, that women in the early church did both pray and prophesy publicly. Philip's four unmarried daughters are given special mention in Acts 21:9, and in his sermon on the day of Pentecost Peter quotes from Joel's prophecy about the prophetic gift that would fall on both men and women (Acts 2:17-18).[6] Of course, as we work out these issues, we need to steer our course carefully between the Scylla of male authoritarianism and the Charybdis of the modern woman's stridency in her appropriation of her church rights — even if biblical texts are produced in support of both views.

When it comes to the organization of the church's life, the New Testament seems to indicate that the work of a deacon was shared by the women. Phoebe clearly exercised this role in the church in Cenchrea.[7] Many also feel that the general word for women in 1 Timothy 3:11 would be more fittingly applied to deaconesses than to the wives of deacons. We do not have a very clear definition of this office, but Phoebe was a woman of some stature, and was commended by Paul to the church in Rome as one who had been 'a great help to many people, including me' (Rom. 16:2). The wisdom and energy of women clearly have a part to play in caring for the life of the church, and it is interesting to note that in Paul's touching greetings to the church in Rome those who are praised for their hard work are all women: Mary, Tryphena, Tryphosa and Persis!

Single women and the church

So far, all that I have said applies to both single and married women. The various facets of the church's life and worship are open to them all in the same way, and the church needs to make sure that this is so. All too often single women, who are already battling with the problems of their own loneliness, feel that they are neglected by the church — even more, possibly, than their single brethren. They sometimes feel that, compared with the security and, as they see it, the social status of the married woman with her home and family base, they are second-class citizens, even in the church. It is important for both the eldership and the church as a whole to show, and at times perhaps emphasize, that this is not the case. Our Lord's teaching in Matthew 19:12 and Paul's statements in 1 Corinthians 7 show that being single is a calling that can be of inestimable value in God's work.

'Huh!', said a single woman cynically at a meeting where that point was made. 'In our church that is usually interpreted as meaning, "Miss B. hasn't got a husband and children, so let's give her as many of the boring jobs as possible. After all, she's got plenty of time".' Perhaps what the church needs to remember is that the single woman needs to be encouraged on the basis of her gifts and abilities, just like any other member, and not on the basis of her singleness. At the same time, she, like the single man, often needs to be helped through the specific problems that singleness brings, just as much as married people need guidance about how to deal with teenagers etc.

Married women

Finally, I do feel increasingly that in the witness of today's local church the married woman has an absolutely vital role to play. This is particularly so in the light of the tragically disintegrating society in which we find ourselves. The family is under attack; more marriages than ever — even Christian ones — are breaking up, and parent-child relationships seem to be at their lowest ebb. Also, as far as the wife and mother are concerned, the pressure upon women to find true fulfilment in outside careers or jobs has meant that the care of home and family is regarded more and more as second-best. It is something that women are sometimes encouraged to endure; after all, it need only be a temporary employment until that moment of liberation arrives when the youngest child goes to school. Not only so, but a growing number of women are leaving their babies and toddlers in day-care centres so that they may continue to work, and they do this not simply to provide necessary extra money for the household.

It is at this point that the married woman member of a local church can step in and show that the care of a husband and family is one of the most wonderful and God-honouring roles open to a woman. It seems to me that this is the point Paul is making in 1 Timothy 2:15. He is saying, in effect, that Eve usurped leadership in the Garden of Eden instead of fulfilling God's purpose for her. Motherhood is God's great unique gift to womankind; let her rejoice and glorify Him in this.

It is not my brief in this chapter to deal with how the Christian woman fulfils her biblical role in the family, but the Christian married woman has a powerful opportunity to show what a wife is meant to be, and that marriage is the God-given basic structure of society. She can show that taking care of children and teaching them is a high and exalted task, and that a woman, whose priority, under God, is her home, can be used in an infinite variety of ways to do His work. The wife portrayed in Proverbs 31 is an example of this — and what an example she is! But this is also soberly underlined by Paul in Titus 2. The older women are to show the younger ones that if women fail in this job, there is a danger that outsiders may 'malign the word of God' (v.5). We need to take this seriously; the cause of the gospel and the ministry of the local church may suffer through our home lives. To quote Lenski: 'The world will to a great extent judge the churches by the character which the gospel produces in the women.'

The importance of a woman's caring ministry is also shown in 1 Timothy 5:10. In today's fractured society, the lonely, the unhappy, the neglected and the suffering can all find a haven in a welcoming home. The listening ear of a woman who is not bound by the times and seasons of a formal job can often be a lifeline to those who need it. How often do we hear from missionaries and inner-city workers that Christian families are some of their most important 'advance troops'! Perhaps this is a lesson for the local church too.

Self-expression, chauvinism, eldership, authority, submission, service, love — all these and many other such terms are whirling around in our minds. More than ever before, perhaps, the Christian woman needs wisdom, and such a wisdom as James describes: 'But the wisdom that comes from heaven is first of all pure; then peace-loving, considerate, submissive, full of mercy and good fruit, impartial and sincere. Peacemakers who sow in peace raise a harvest of righteousness' (James 3:17-18).

God grant that we may have a double portion of this wisdom, and that we women in the local church may live to God's glory, in obedience to His Word.

NOTES

1 The film *Kramer v. Kramer* explores this problem, and that of the father, in a moving and balanced way.
2 David Field, 'Headship in Marriage: The Husband's View', in *The Role of Women* ed. by S. Lees (Inter-Varsity Press, 1984), p.46.
3 John Stott, *The Message of Ephesians* (Inter-Varsity Press, 1979), p.221.
4 It is probably not accidental that Priscilla's name precedes her husband's in the account of their teaching role (Acts 18:26).
5 For a description of the agony of mind that this can cause, see Margaret Manton's two articles in *The Evangelical Magazine of Wales* 20.3,4 (1981).
6 It is not part of my brief in this chapter to discuss the continuance or cessation of the gifts.
7 She is described by the word *diakonos* (Rom. 16:1).

QUESTIONS FOR DISCUSSION

a) Consider the Scripture passages referred to in the section 'Male and Female Differences?'. How far are our own attitudes wrongly influenced by either past tradition or the Women's Movement?

b) List everything in your church that is done by (i) men and (ii) women. Can you justify this division of labour from Scripture?

c) Using Shirley Lees' book, *The Role of Women,* read the chapters that you are most likely to disagree with. In discussion, identify the main strengths and weaknesses of the writers' arguments.

d) What problems arise in applying biblical teaching on the role of women in a missionary situation?

FURTHER READING

A. Atkins, *Split Image* (Hodder & Stoughton, 1987)
M. J. Evans, *Woman in the Bible* (Paternoster, 1983)
J. Hurley *Man and Woman in Biblical Perspective* (Inter-Varsity Press, 1981)
M. Langley, *Equal Woman* (Marshalls, 1983)
S. Lees (ed.), *The Role of Women* (Inter-Varsity Press, 1984)
J. R. Richards, *The Sceptical Feminist* (Penguin, 1982)
E. Storkey, *What's Right with Feminism?* (SPCK, 1985)

Commentaries are particularly useful on this subject:

W. Hendriksen, *Timothy and Titus* (Banner of Truth, 1964)

C. Hodge, *1 Corinthians* (Banner of Truth, 1974)

R. C. H. Lenski, *Interpretation of St Paul's Epistles: Colossians-Philemon* (Wartburg Press, n.d.)

D. M. Lloyd-Jones, *Life in the Spirit* (Banner of Truth, 1974)

D. Prior, *The Message of 1 Corinthians* (Inter-Varsity Press, 1985)

J. Stott, *God's New Society: The Message of Ephesians* (Inter-Varsity Press, 1979)

9

Social Welfare and the Local Church

PETER MILSOM and IAN SHAW

The Bible repeatedly pleads for Christians to show active concern for the welfare of the socially needy and vulnerable members of society and the church. 'Wash and make yourselves clean', reasons Isaiah. 'Take your evil deeds out of my sight! Stop doing wrong, learn to do right! Seek justice, encourage the oppressed. Defend the cause of the fatherless, plead the cause of the widow' (Isa. 1:16-17). 'I hate, I despise your religious feasts', says the Lord through Amos. 'I cannot stand your assemblies . . . Let justice roll on like a river, righteousness like a never-failing stream!' (Amos 5:21,24). The promise is that under the gospel 'the eyes of the blind will be opened and the ears of the deaf unstopped. Then will the lame leap like a deer, and the tongue of the dumb shout for joy' (Isa. 35:5,6). While this must be widened to include the spiritually blind and deaf (Isa. 42:18-19; 43:8; Matt. 15:14; John 9:39), the physically handicapped must not be excluded.

Pleas for social welfare and justice are not restricted to the prophets. The law of Moses urges concern for the immigrant, the poor, the deaf, the blind, the fatherless, the widow and the servant (Ex. 23:9; Lev. 19; Deut. 10:18-19; 15:7-18).

When we turn to the New Testament, we find that the Christian is exhorted to have a preserving effect on the whole of society as a witness to our Father in heaven (Matt. 5:13-16). The state is not only to punish evil, but also to encourage good (Rom. 13:3-6; 1 Pet. 2:13-14). Although the Christian's concern is to be demonstrated first in the 'household of faith' and in his or her own family, it is not to stop there, but to extend to all people (Acts 4:32-35; Gal. 6:10; 1 Thess. 3:12; 5:15; 1 Tim. 5:4,8). We are to imitate our heavenly Father, who sends the blessings of sun and rain on the righteous and unrighteous alike (Matt. 5:44-45).

EVANGELICAL HESITATION

In the face of such biblical exhortations, why have Christians, until recently, displayed evident uncertainty in their commitment to social welfare? The uncertainty is not inherent in the evangelical faith itself. For example, Jonathan Edwards, who was not a man to use words lightly, wrote:

> It is . . . our bounden duty, as much a duty as it is to pray, or to attend public worship, or any thing else whatever . . . I know of scarce any duty which is so much insisted on, so pressed and urged upon us both in the Old Testament and New, as this duty of charity to the poor.[1]

Indeed, in their recognition of the vital importance of this activity in the life of the church, some Christians, particularly in the Scottish Presbyterian tradition, have regarded the demonstration of practical compassion ('distributions', to use the old-fashioned terminology) as an essential part of a true New Testament church.[2]

Three connected reasons can be suggested for the uncertainty to which we have just referred. First, we are heirs to an evangelical reaction against the 'social gospel' of the late nineteenth and early twentieth centuries. In addition, there is no strong recent tradition of biblical thinking on social welfare issues to guide our involvement. Finally, in Western democracies, the twentieth century has seen an enormous growth in the welfare activities of the state. As a result, in seeking to establish a biblical response to welfare issues, post-war Britain has been facing a dramatically different set of questions from those faced by earlier generations. Those questions are equally acute, though in some respects different, whether Christians are endeavouring to fashion their response through the local church, voluntary organizations, or as employees of the state.

'The spirit of social work is the spirit of the Sermon on the Mount.'[3] This was until fairly recently the belief of many people who were religiously inclined and involved in welfare work. The Christian Socialists, with their belief in the universal brotherhood of man, derived socialist principles from the Sermon on the Mount. Their doctrine of divine immanence held no place for any distinction between the sacred and the secular, and it supported their desire for a kingdom of God on earth. As observers at the time were well aware, social questions became the vital questions of the day, and these took the place of religion.

In the light of these developments evangelicals tended to withdraw from social involvement and even to attack it. Billy Sunday, the American evangelist, is reported to have complained, 'We've had enough of this godless social service nonsense!'[4] While the evangelical hesitation about welfare issues may have been regrettable, it needs to be reaffirmed that it was entirely understandable, and the derogatory tone of some evangelical writers on this theme is unfortunate. However, this withdrawal has left Christians without a recent tradition of thoroughgoing biblical thought and action and has exposed them to the danger of being drawn by views which have little claim to being biblical. Indeed, having reacted against the deficiencies of 'fundamentalism', some evangelical writers run the risk of regarding the evil of theological liberalism as less dangerous than it really is, and of treating fundamentalism and liberalism as roughly equivalent evils.

THE BIBLE ON SOCIAL WELFARE

It is a central theme of this book that social issues cannot be simply tacked on to the gospel or responded to in a separate compartment. If that is allowed to happen, the Christian's social concern will either fade away to insignificance or become disproportionate and unbiblical in its importance, producing uncertainty and confusion because Christians are faced with a multiplicity of competing claims on their witness. Social welfare is part and parcel of the Bible's teaching about creation, the fall of man and redemption. In each case, these biblical themes provide part of the motive for social concern, and at the same time give clear general principles indicating the direction in which Christians are to go when applying the teaching. Having given attention in the first part of this book to the general teaching of the Bible on social issues, we suggest here ways in which the biblical teaching about creation, the fall of man and redemption have a particular bearing on social welfare.

Creation

God made man in His own image, and He gave certain commands which were not cancelled by the Fall. Marriage, employment, care for the weak, and so on, are to be governed by how God made us. If this is so, then these divine demands apply to all indiscriminately, and provide a good ground upon which the Christian and the non-Christian can stand together.

There are clear examples of such reasoning in the Bible. Job was quite right, when pleading his case against his friends, to reflect as follows:

137

> If I have denied justice to my menservants and maidservants when they had a grievance against me, what will I do when God confronts me? What will I answer when called to account? Did not he who made me in the womb make them? Did not the same one form us both within our mothers?
>
> Job 31:13-15

The members of his household had the right to fair dealing and concern for their welfare, not because Job was a believer, true as that was, but because of their common humanity in the sight of God. 'Rich and poor have this in common: the Lord is the Maker of them all' (Prov. 22:2). Thus, 'he who oppresses the poor shows contempt for their Maker' (Prov. 14:31; cf. 17:5; 19:17).

A helpful example of the outworking of this principle is seen in the various passages in the Old Testament where the prophets declare God's judgment on the sins of the pagan nations surrounding Israel (e.g. Ezek. 25-32; Amos 1:1-2:5; Jer. 46-51; Isa. 13-24; Zeph. 2). On what grounds can God reprove and judge these nations? They are not God's children, so no appeal can be made to them as believers; neither has God's revelation been given to them. We must conclude that God's judgment falls upon these nations because 'the requirements of the law are written on their hearts' (Rom. 2:15), and they have violated their consciences which have borne witness against their sins. By and large God reproves them for social sins — sins of human relationships. Pride, breach of promise, placing commercial profit above human welfare, being worldly-minded, seeking their own advantage, taking revenge, harbouring unlimited ambition, treating people as if they were things, and so on — all these sins are mentioned.[5]

If God judges men and women for the breach of these principles, the Christian today can appeal to the non-Christian to collaborate in the upholding of these same values, knowing that such an appeal will receive an authenticating assent in the conscience of the unbeliever. (At the same time he must beware of naive optimism in imagining that far-reaching or permanent social improvement can be achieved.) Christ gives a striking, if incidental, confirmation of this truth in His teaching about prayer:

> Which of you, if his son asks for bread, will give him a stone? Or if he asks for a fish, will give him a snake? If you then, *though you are evil,* know how to give good gifts to your children, how much more will your Father in heaven give good gifts to those who ask him!
>
> Matthew 7:9-11 (cf. Matt. 5:46-47; Luke 6:32-34; John 15:19)

Reasoning from the greater to the less, Christ finds irrefutable logic in the premise that sinful parents are capable of good. The account

138

of Paul's journey to Rome also illustrates the kindness which unbelievers may show to others (e.g. Acts 27:43; 28:1-10). In the perfect providence of God, such creation structures make possible the day-by-day survival of human society.

The Fall

Scripture, however, does not stop at this point. It is totally insufficient to argue, as some have done, that a strong doctrine of the image of God in man, allied to the renewal accomplished in Christ, is a sufficient basis for Christian welfare ethics. It can only lead to an over-optimistic view of human nature. True, 'when God created man, he made him in the likeness of God' (Gen. 5:1), and remnants of that likeness survived the Fall. However, 'when Adam had lived 130 years, he had a son in *his own* likeness, in *his own* image' (Gen. 5:3). We live in a fallen, non-ideal world, and this complicates the application of God's righteous law. Our eternal duties are clear and absolute: repent, believe, witness, etc. But past wrongs have often created situations in which whatever we do in regard to temporal duties is flawed by sin. Moral dilemmas have been discussed in the first chapter, and situations of this kind are increasingly common in our churches.

How are we to behave in such circumstances? We must work for the situation that is the nearest possible to God's ideal. The lesser evil — or, more properly, the greater good — then becomes our duty. The Old Testament teaching on divorce provides an example of this (Deut. 24:1-4; cf. Ezra 10:9-15; Matt. 19:1-9).

How are we to determine the greater good in any given situation? The following questions may serve as tests of the rightness of our advice or help:[6]

1. Does our action recognize God's absolute standards? Does it seek to unify the person's duty and happiness?
2. Would our action make a good general rule?
3. Will it prevent or hinder a recurrence of the problem?
4. Would our action help or harm conscience? Will it, implicitly at least, lead to a clearer view of God's standards?
5. Does our action aim to restore God's ideals as much as possible?
6. Does it foster acceptance of personal responsibility and duty?

Redemption

Creation ethics do not exhaust the Christian's motives for social concern. In addition, we are to be merciful because as Christians we have ourselves received mercy (Luke 6:36). This is clearly taught throughout Scripture. In requiring that God's people should show concern for the welfare of vulnerable members of society, Moses usually appealed to the fact that they had been on the receiving end of God's incomparable grace. The demand not to oppress the immigrant, but to love him as themselves, is repeatedly reinforced with the reminder that 'you yourselves know how it feels to be aliens, because you were aliens in Egypt' (Exod. 23:9; cf. Lev. 19:34; Deut. 10:19). Precisely similar reasoning is employed to show what their attitude should be to servants and other people at risk of exploitation: 'remember that you were slaves in Egypt and the Lord your God redeemed you from there' (Deut. 24:18).

To be labelled a 'do-gooder' is not something most of us would welcome, but in Jesus it was a clear evidence of the anointing of the Holy Spirit (Acts 10:38). The same was doubtless true of Dorcas (Acts 9:36), whose life exemplified the truth that religion is both worship and behaviour. Pure and faultless religion, says James, includes the duty 'to look after orphans and widows in their distress' (James 1:27). This is only the practical outworking of being 'created in Christ Jesus to do good works' (Eph. 2:10).

Thus, while there are ample grounds for Christians and non-Christians to collaborate in welfare activities, it is the death of Christ in our place that constitutes for the Christian the supreme motivation for exercising himself in social welfare.[7] Christ 'gave himself for us to redeem us from all wickedness and to purify for himself a people that are his very own, eager to do what is good' (Titus 2:14). 'You know the grace of our Lord Jesus Christ', reasons the apostle, 'that though he was rich, yet for your sakes he became poor, so that you through his poverty might become rich' (2 Cor. 8:9). Why does Paul make this great statement about the work of Christ? To provide a motive for the Corinthians to give to needy Christians, so that great inequalities between believers might be removed. Christians are sometimes found echoing Poor Law thinking about the deserving and the undeserving poor. If we are to take this injunction seriously, and imperfectly model our welfare activities on the Saviour's work, we will not restrict our efforts to those who are appreciative or 'deserving' of our contribution.

SOCIAL WELFARE AND EVANGELISM

What is the relationship between social welfare activities and evangelism? Should the local church as such be involved in welfare initiatives, or is this something which should be left to the individual? If particular churches are to be active, how might different churches collaborate with and support one another? Is involvement in social welfare an obligation for everyone in the church, or only for certain people? These are some of the questions which arise from our discussion so far. In the remainder of the chapter we will attempt to answer them, and conclude with brief case studies to illustrate how particular churches have endeavoured to respond to the Bible's teaching.

There are some faithful Christians who feel that any kind of social action by the believer is suspect. The eternal destiny of the soul is the only thing that matters, they will argue. How can we afford to spend our fleeting time in any activity which does not face people directly with the claims of the gospel? Linked to this is the fear that social involvement will make us lukewarm Christians and draw us into a mixture of legalism and the distorted agenda of liberal theology.

The 'lukewarm Christian' argument cannot stand up to scrutiny. Whatever may have happened to the spiritual life of some professing Christians who are socially active, there is nothing inherent in demonstrations of social compassion that hinders Christian living. On the contrary, Scripture gives ample encouragement to the belief that spiritual blessing is promised to those who faithfully carry out this responsibility (Deut. 15:10; Prov. 11:24-25; 28:27; Matt. 10:42; Luke 14:13-14; 2 Cor. 9:6-8; 1 Tim. 6:17-19).

The cleavage between social concern and evangelism cannot be sustained from Scripture either. Evangelism and social concern are distinct from one another, but they are also to be closely integrated. In the Bible, the integral relationship of evangelism and social concern is often implied rather than stated. In the Sermon on the Mount, Christ talks of giving to the needy and of prayer (Matt. 6:1-15). Here we have examples of 'social' and 'spiritual' duties; the two stand side by side and, more strikingly, in support of each duty an appeal is made to precisely the same principles of right motives and true rewards. This amounts to a most compelling assumption of the unity of Christian worship and witness.

Again, in the miracle of the feeding of the five thousand, Christ says to the disciples, '*You* give them something to eat' (Mark 6:37). 'Do not think as the world thinks', He seems to be saying; 'You have access to a source of help that should enable you to deal with problems that the world cannot solve.' Presumably there *were* ordinary means of supply, as the disciples suggested, but man's extremity is the Christian's opportunity. Christ did not allow the disciples to draw a neat line between evangelism and social concern, nor did He tell them to act in a purely personal capacity and to share their personal provisions. Instead, He led them to make a corporate response to a particular situation in order to demonstrate that His compassion for the people extended to the most basic of physical needs.

The relationship between social concern and evangelism may take three different forms. First, social concern sometimes follows on as a consequence of evangelism (Gal. 5:6; James 2:18; 1 John 3:16ff.), and may even be part of the aim of evangelism (James 2:14ff.). Secondly, social concern may be a bridge to evangelism. The case studies at the end of the chapter illustrate how social concern may gain a hearing for the gospel, and Christ on occasions performed works of mercy before proclaiming the gospel. Finally, social concern may act as a partner with evangelism. In Christ's ministry 'His words explained his works, and his works dramatised his words'.[8] Evangelism may have social implications, and social concern may have evangelistic implications. They are therefore distinct but integrally related.

On very rare occasions there may be tensions between the two. If this happens, evangelism must be primary (e.g. Acts 6). 'What is seen is temporary, what is unseen is eternal' (2 Cor. 4:18). When, in the sequel to the feeding of the five thousand, the people continued to follow Him and displayed an obvious neglect of their spiritual plight, Jesus spoke strongly to them:

> I tell you the truth, you are looking for me, not because you saw miraculous signs but because you ate the loaves and had your fill. Do not work for food that spoils, but for the food that endures to eternal life, which the Son of Man will give you. On him God the Father has placed his seal of approval. John 6:26-27

So too, in ministering to people's physical needs, Christians must never be afraid to speak clearly when they see people stopping short of eternal realities.

Observing Mary's anointing of Jesus, Judas and others complained that the money she had spent on perfume could have been given to the poor. The Lord replied, 'The poor you will always have with you, and you can help them any time you want. But you will not always have me' (Mark 14:7). This verse must not be interpreted, however, as an excuse for neglecting temporal needs. Christ is quoting from Deuteronomy, and in the original context the continuing existence of poverty is used to encourage generosity rather than to condone *laissez-faire* indifference. 'There will always be poor people in the land. *Therefore* I command you to be open-handed towards your brothers and towards the poor and needy in your land' (Deut. 15:11). Rather than competing with one another, social concern and evangelism should work together in the life and witness of our churches in a mutually supportive spiral of increasing concern.

THE LOCAL CHURCH AND SOCIAL ACTION

The church is central in all God's purposes. Each local church is in a real sense the hub from which God's activity radiates. Its members are organically united to Christ their living Head, and through Him are joined to each other. The life of Christ is present in the local church as a whole, and in each particular member of it. These basic truths provide guidelines for answering a question which often arises in connection with the local church's involvement in social action, namely, Is social action a legitimate area of concern for a local church as a church? Behind the question lies a desire to ensure that the church is not deflected from its primary task of proclaiming the gospel of the Lord Jesus Christ. The latter is seen to be the proper task of the church as a church, and social action is regarded as a province for individual action alone.

While it is recognized that in some areas — politics at national and local level, for instance — it would be inappropriate for the church to act as a body, does this mean that a co-ordinated response to particular social needs is never to be made by a local church? Indeed, ought any individual Christian ever to lose sight of his organic union with his fellow Christians? A local church should be more organic than institutional. This will be true not only when its members gather together for worship or for a church meeting, but every day in their life in the community. All actions are taken in the context of fellowship with our fellow believers and in dependence on their encouragement and prayers.

The vital organic nature of the church should express itself in every aspect of its life — worship, fellowship, evangelism and service. Social welfare, therefore, should not be viewed as a purely individual matter. The preaching and teaching of the church should encourage Christians in their daily lives in the world, focusing attention on the twin activities of God-centred worship and Christlike service. Local churches should be 'ministry-centred' (that is, 'service-centred') as well as 'meeting-centred'.

The local church should be the normal base for such an expression of Christian concern, and Christian agencies the exception. The service of Christians in the local church serves a twofold purpose: first, to express God's love to those outside the church; secondly, to help those within the church to become mature Christians, and to strengthen their commitment to Christian service.

143

Both these areas should be goals of the ministry of the church as a whole.

Churches who respond to social needs must always maintain their priorities clearly. The needs of people at large are overwhelming and are capable of swamping the resources of any local congregation. Where possible, co-operation between local churches will strengthen the ministry of caring. The pooling of resources, human, material and spiritual, will enable a Christian response to be made in situations which are beyond any one local church. In the area of unemployment, for example, one congregation may have only a few unemployed members, who consequently feel isolated: another may have so many that it is unable to cope with the need. A joint response to such problems by a number of churches would assist greatly.

A WORLD OF NEED

We live in a world full of needy people. Every community manifests this need. The more we get to know people's situations, the more conscious we become of how great the need is. In Britain the state welfare provision makes a substantial contribution towards the meeting of the need in terms of personnel and financial resources, but this would be significantly enhanced by a caring, devoted Christian response. The apostolic injunction, 'Therefore, as we have opportunity, let us do good to *all* people, especially to those who belong to the family of believers' (Gal. 6:10), continues to be very relevant. Here the word 'good' includes the idea of 'beautiful'. The practical expression of Christian love is a means of bringing beauty into lives which are often disfigured by sin and misery. Christians have a duty to all, and especially to each other. The parable of the good Samaritan makes it clear that a narrow definition of who our 'neighbour' is must be rejected. The command to love extends to all, even to our personal enemies. Such caring will often involve inconvenience and cost in terms of time and money (Luke 10:25-37; cf. Matt. 5:43-48; Rom. 12:17-21).

We have already argued that evangelism and social concern should not be regarded as two totally separate areas of activity. In many cases evangelism will lead us to cases of social need. All full-orbed Christian social concern keeps in view the responsibility to be ambassadors for the gospel. The so-called 'social gospel' lacked clear convictions regarding man's spiritual plight and urgent need to be reconciled to God through Christ. There is no biblical reason why those who are totally committed to proclaiming Christ to the

144

lost cannot also be deeply committed to social action. In fact, we may need to take a long, hard look at our evangelism. Does our desire to make Christ known lead us into meaningful relationships with people in the community around us, or do we prefer a 'hit-and-run' approach which stops short of whole-hearted commitment to those whom we seek to evangelize?

Caring for the whole person

We are to care for the *whole* person. It is wrong to care for the body and neglect the soul, but it is also wrong to care for the soul and neglect the body. As Christians reach out to their community they inevitably discover people in need, and their needs are often long-term, deep-seated and complicated. Their greatest need is to find peace with God through Jesus Christ, but their other needs are also very real and cry out for Christian compassion. Are we only to become involved in seeking to meet these needs if we judge that the people are 'genuine seekers'? Will we only help them if they start to attend church services, or should Christian love find expression without strings attached?

Broadly speaking, our concern should be for those whom the New Testament describes as 'poor' (e.g. Luke 1:52-53; 4:18; 6:20-36; 7:22): in other words, those who are in need on grounds of health, poverty, social stigma, etc., and who also have no spiritual pretensions or claims on God. In the case of Christ's ministry this included Gentiles, lepers, widows and immoral women. Therefore, on our part, we are to give 'without expecting to get anything back' (Luke 6:35). When we say that the gospel is for the poor, we are reminding ourselves that the gospel is a message of grace, and our social welfare activities should always serve to undergird that truth.

Using God-given gifts

Within the local congregation there is a rich variety of God-given talents and gifts. In addition to natural endowments, some Christians have pursued specialized training and gained experience in areas of social concern. Others, though they lack training and expertise, have a special interest and concern in certain areas and also have gifts of service to others (Acts 6:1-6; Rom. 12:6-8; 1 Pet. 4:10-11). In all cases, if such concern is genuine, it will find expression in the individual's life and daily contact with people. Those with appropriate qualifications may work within state welfare, thus making a valuable Christian contribution to that service.

The question arises as to whether there is another legitimate avenue, between the statutory provisions and individual activity. Is

145

it biblically justified to engage in church-based social action, which is independent of the state provision but is more than a purely personal undertaking? We believe it is. An individual Christian could undertake social action in a specific area of need, under the authority of the eldership, in conjunction with the diaconate, and with the support of the whole congregation. Such an approach arises from a clear sense of personal call which is evident to and ratified by the whole congregation.

The biblical office of the deacon has been seriously neglected by Christians. The word 'deacon' is almost a transliteration of the Greek words used in the New Testament for 'serving' and 'service'. For the Christian, service is the very thing that marks a person out as a disciple of Christ. When the disciples argued together about which of them was the leader, Christ gave them an understanding of service which went completely contrary to the view of the world accepted by Jews and Greeks alike.

> Jesus said to them, 'The kings of the Gentiles lord it over them; and those who exercise authority over them call themselves Benefactors. But you are not to be like that. Instead, the greatest among you should be like the youngest, and the one who rules like the one who serves . . . I am among you as one who serves.'   Luke 22:25-27 (cf. John 13:1-17)

Those who hold the office of deacon should exemplify the very heart of the gospel message. Sadly, not all do so. We urgently need a fresh realization of the extent of biblical teaching on giving to the needy, or 'diaconal' giving (2 Cor. 8; 9), the institution of a genuine weekly 'diaconal' offering (1 Cor. 16:2), and a thorough-going commitment to biblical, pro-active compassion. There is a very real sense in which every Christian is a deacon and should engage in diaconal service. At the judgment-seat Christ will ask everyone whether they did the work of a deacon (Matt. 25:31-46).

Unlike state provision, church-based work of this kind does not necessarily involve heavy financial commitment. Indeed it may not require much at all in the way of financial resources from the church, but it is strong in personal commitment and motivation. The Christian involved may be willing to forgo a full salary and live instead on income received from part-time employment, spending the rest of his or her time in pursuing church-based social activity. This would involve an element of personal sacrifice similar to the apostle Paul's tent-making. Alternatively, where possible and appropriate, the local congregation could provide financial support, thus freeing the individual to give more time to the work. It is important that such church-based social activity should supplement and complement other expressions of social concern in the congregation as a whole and not be seen as a substitute for it. The ministry of the Word is intended 'to prepare God's people for works of service' (Eph. 4:12), not to excuse them from such service. The eldership should support and counsel the individual doing the work, and ensure that everything is done in keeping with biblical principles and the highest standards. Other Christians in the congregation also have a vital role. Some may be able to assist, others can encourage, and all can pray.

Whatever our particular response, God grant that we may be biblical not only in what we do, but also in how we do it! May we show concern ungrudgingly (Isa. 58:10; Deut. 15:10; 2 Cor. 9:7), from a pure motive (Matt. 6:3), generously (Deut. 15:11; Rom. 12:8; 1 Tim. 6:18), without delay (Prov. 3:27,28), and (though never content to stop short at that point) beginning in our own families and among the fellowship of believers (Acts 4:32-35; Gal. 6:10; 1 Thess. 3:12; 5:15; 1 Tim. 5:4,8).

CHURCH-BASED SOCIAL WELFARE: EXAMPLES

1. Mental handicap

A qualified teacher, experienced in teaching the mentally handicapped and working in a residential care setting, became a member of a church of approximately 60 members. Her growing convictions about the limitations of work in schools and residential homes, the fact that she had a younger brother with Down's Syndrome, and the interest of the church, all contributed to the setting up of a work within the church. She has been supported financially by the church, and over a six-year period she has made significant contact with more than 30 local families.

The work takes the form of personal visiting and regular parents' meetings. Individual families in the church have been linked with familes who have a mentally handicapped child. Bible teaching aids are being prepared specifically for those with a mental handicap. One parent has been converted, and others regularly attend the services. Through this ministry the whole congregation has been made aware of the demands of caring for a mentally handicapped person, and many families previously outside the church have experienced Christian love and heard the gospel of Jesus Christ.

2. Community work

A man with a background in social work is employed by a Midlands church as a full-time community worker. He and his wife live in a flat adjoining the church premises. His work is not structured in any definite way, although he is a member of the eldership and has regular meetings with the minister. Over the last two years a number of activities have developed, with varying degrees of success, including a mums and toddlers group, welfare rights advice, and a Bible study and prayer support group consisting of about five West Indian ladies.

The general aims are to provide a community service aimed at bringing church members into contact with local people and building bridges in relationships with them. It is the prayer of the church that the project will give opportunity for the proclamation of the gospel as well as works of love and service. The church building is sited in an inner-city area, with all its attendant problems, and the response has not always been very positive. It is hoped that Christian families, couples and single people in the church will deliberately move into the area.

3. Terminal illness

This project began after a married woman with two young children was converted. She is a trained nurse, and soon after her conversion her husband developed a brain tumour and died within a year. Her experience of caring for her husband at home, and of knowing the sustaining grace of God in that situation, made her very conscious of the great need of those facing a similar situation but without a personal knowledge of God. In consultation with the elders at her local church she began a ministry to individuals and families facing terminal illness, and after a few months received financial support from the church.

For various reasons contact was not easy to establish, but over a period of six years many good opportunities have been presented, mainly through the personal contacts of Christians. The work requires close involvement with families as they go through times of great difficulty and deep distress, and the worker seeks to give practical support and care, warm friendship, and spiritual ministry through the Word of God and prayer. The personal demands of such work are great, both emotionally and spiritually. Many families have appreciated the human and divine support they have received, and more than one has come to faith through this ministry.

NOTES

1 Jonathan Edwards, 'Christian Charity', in *Works* (Banner of Truth, 1974), p.164.
2 Quoted from *The Second Book of Discipline,* chapter 11, by Donald MacLeod in 'The Basis of Christian Unity', *Evangel,* 3.3 (1985).
3 Quoted from Ernest Devine by M. E. Marty in 'Social Service: Godly and Godless', *Social Service Review,* 54 (1980).
4 M. E. Marty, 'Social Service: Godly and Godless'.
5 Sins of human relationship are, of course, one cause of God's judgment upon Israel and Judah as well as the pagan nations. Also, God does occasionally reprove the pagan nations for sins of spiritual unbelief (e.g. Hab. 2:18-20). But the general point we have made still stands. See J. A. Motyer, *The Message of Amos* (Inter-Varsity Press, 1974), pp. 35-68.
6 These guidelines were first suggested by Robert Horn in a paper on 'The Lesser Evil: Moral Choice in a Non-ideal World'.
7 Scripture does not keep creation ethics and redemption ethics in separate, water-tight compartments, but frequently brings them together. For example, Malachi on divorce (Mal. 2:15), Paul on marriage (Eph. 5:22-24), and Paul to Philemon about Onesimus (Philem. 15-16).
8 *Evangelism and Social Responsibility* — the Lausanne Conference Report (Paternoster, 1982), p.23.

QUESTIONS FOR DISCUSSION AND ACTION

a) (i) What is the biblical relationship between evangelism and social concern? Consider, for example, Matthew 5:13-16; 6:1-15; Mark 6:30-44; 14:3-11 (Deuteronomy 15:11); John 6:26f.; Acts 6:1-7; James 2:14-26; 1 John 3:16-20.
Scripture references should be given out to group members a week in advance. Spend 30-45 minutes on this part of the question.

(ii) In small groups of 3-5 members, spend 30 minutes identifying ways in which this teaching applies to your local church or Christian group. Share your results with the whole group.

b) What are the main characteristics of Christian serving? Consider Matthew 25:31-46; Luke 12:35-38; 22:24-27; Mark 10:41-45; John 13:1-17; Acts 6:1-7; Romans 12:6-8; Galatians 6:10; 1 Timothy 3:8-13; 5:3-10.
How are we to implement a diaconal ministry in our church/group and community?

c) If someone in your group has had the experience of being on the receiving end of 'care' of any kind, or has been closely associated with someone who has, ask them to share honestly with the group their response to that experience. What can we learn from this as Christians?

FURTHER READING

The general principles considered in the first part of this chapter can be followed up through the reading recommended for the early chapters of this book. Perhaps the most thoughtful reading on the relation of evangelism and social concern can be found in the Lausanne Conference Report, *Evangelism and Social Responsibility* (Paternoster, 1982). The responsibilities of deacons for social welfare are thoroughly considered by Leonard Coppes in *Who Will Lead Us?* (Pilgrim Publishing House, 1977), chapters 10-13. The fullest discussion of the work of deacons is found in Peter Y. de Yong's book *The Ministry of Mercy for Today* (Baker, 1952). Practical challenges to Christians regarding fostering and adoption and handicapped children have been presented by Stuart Olyott and David Potter in *Christian Family Matters* edited by Ian Shaw (Evangelical Press of Wales, 1985). Charles Spurgeon's church took many social initiatives which, while we would not wish to copy them in detail, provide a spiritual stimulus to us in working out our own responsibilities. A good recent account can be read in Arnold Dallimore's biography of Spurgeon (Banner of Truth, 1985). Thomas Chalmers undertook one of the most considered nineteenth-century initiatives in the field of social welfare through the local church. A good account of his work can be read in Stewart Brown's *Thomas Chalmers and the Godly Commonwealth* (Oxford University Press, 1982).

10

The Church and its Mission in the Contemporary World

DAVID SMITH

Many evangelical Christians today appear to be both confused and discouraged with regard to the work of mission. On the one hand, they are convinced that the commission of Christ to evangelize the nations remains binding. Indeed, this conviction is integral to evangelical self-understanding: to be an evangelical is to be committed to mission. The roots of contemporary evangelicalism lie deep in the era which saw the birth of the modern missionary movement, so that we feel ourselves to be heirs of a tradition which includes names like Carey, Hudson Taylor and C.T. Studd. Yet, on the other hand, this ineradicable missionary impulse seems to be continually frustrated in the modern world by a complex web of factors, which inhibit the actual practice of missions. We hear of 'doors closing', of entry visas being refused, of experienced missionaries being asked to leave areas in which they have worked for years. The traditional fields no longer seem to be 'white to harvest'; in many cases they are now fenced off and placarded with notices reading 'Out of bounds!' In this situation the Western Christian faces a painful dilemma: he is sure that the support of missions is no optional extra but belongs to the essence of Christian obedience; yet he cannot close his eyes to the reality of a world in which the outworking of this obedience seems to become ever more difficult.

I want to suggest where a primary source of this confusion and discouragement may lie. I believe that a basic evangelical conviction concerning the irrevocable nature of the church's missionary obligation has become entangled with a mistaken adherence to an outdated method of fulfilling that obligation. It is nearly two hundred years since William Carey published his *Enquiry*. That work was remarkable not because of its theological insights, but because of its detailed survey of the state of the world and its insistence upon the need to devise 'means' for evangelization. Carey's little

151

book was essentially pragmatic; he demanded that his contemporaries face up to the question of *how* the church might fulfil its missionary calling. It seems to me that we must confront Carey's question anew today. We must examine the world as it really is, abandon outmoded images of peoples and nations, and plan a strategy of mission which relates to the true need of the world at the close of the twentieth century. Following Carey, we must ask which 'means' are appropriate to the task of mission today. In 1792 Carey answered that question with the revolutionary proposal that a voluntary society should be formed. It may well be that we, two centuries later, are required to devise means for evangelizing our generation which may appear at first glance to be equally revolutionary.

THE TASK FACING THE CHURCH TODAY

Clearly it is not possible within the limited scope of this chapter to provide a detailed description and analysis of the contemporary situation. Besides, this has been done elsewhere. Patrick Johnstone's *Operation World: A Handbook for World Intercession* surveys the whole earth and contains much valuable information. Even more detailed is David Barrett's monumental *World Christian Encyclopedia*. The very existence of works such as these points to a contrast between the age of Carey and our own. Carey gathered as much information as he could lay his hands upon, but, compared to the resources available to us today, his knowledge was extremely limited. Yet, if this seems to give us an advantage, the facts known to us concerning the spiralling growth in world population and the seemingly uncontrolled increase in just about every category of human need confront us with the stark reality of the unfinished task of mission.

Commenting on his own statistics concerning the growth in numbers of urban dwellers (one million *per week*) and the increase in the hungry and starving (calculated at over 1.5 billion people), Barrett observes that, for the Christian who cares about God's world and his mission in it, the sheer magnitude of numerical increase in all these areas 'has already become a global nightmare'.[1] In relation to religious allegiances Barrett's figures will immediately dispel any smug and facile confidence that the task of mission is over. Muslims increase by 17 million a year; Hindus by 12 million; Buddhists by 4 million. One of the most striking statistics of all, and one which, as we shall see, has particular implication for mission in the Western world, concerns the growth in the numbers of people described as 'non-religious' or 'atheist'. In 1900 there were approximately 3 million such people; today the figure is almost 1,017 million and rising fast. Of course, statistics can be misleading and they can be misused. However, no Christian who is sensitive to the needs of the world and the glory of God can possibly ignore the immense challenge of these facts. Surely we are still 'facing a task unfinished that drives [or should drive] us to our knees'.

In thinking about the Christian mission in the world today it may be helpful to identify a number of distinct types of situation, each of which demands special thought and action. I do not claim that the following list is exhaustive, but it may help us, in confronting the challenge of mission at the end of the twentieth century, to think about missiological priorities and methods in relation to such a schema.

Mission accomplished!

There are many areas of traditional missionary activity where it is possible to say — and to say with rejoicing — 'Mission accomplished!' There is a crucial distinction to be drawn between 'mission' in its broadest sense, which is a task which will remain incomplete until the return of Christ, and 'missions' of a particular and localized kind which do, or should, come to an end. Indeed, missions of this second kind can only be judged successful in so far as they are completed. Mission, in this sense, is *finishable*. The objective of missions is to plant the seed of the gospel in alien soil and to see it spring to life in the form of young, indigenous churches. How long it will take to achieve this objective will depend on many factors: in some cases the preaching of Christ will bear immediate fruit; in others inhospitable soil will demand long years of labour. However, whether short or long, once the goal is achieved we may declare, 'Mission accomplished!' — and we may do so not with regret and despondency, as though the end of mission represented failure on our part, but with great joy and thankfulness to God. This, at any rate, seems to be the apostolic view of missions. Paul and Barnabas went back to Antioch, having seen their preaching bear fruit in the planting of young churches, and they reported with evident rejoicing on the work 'they had now completed' (Acts 14:26). The door of faith was now open to the Gentiles, the 'mission' was over and the evangelists could now turn their attention to new regions beyond. Ideally, therefore, the history of missions should be punctuated by the cry, 'Mission is dead; long live mission!'

This is not to say that young churches are to be abandoned by older churches and left to themselves. On the contrary, Paul's deep conviction as to the catholicity of the church meant that he always and everywhere insisted on the fundamental oneness of all believers and laboured to ensure that churches expressed true fellowhip across geographical and cultural boundaries. Such fellowship, however, does not occur within the context of mission; it is, rather, the expression of the unity of different parts of the body of Christ and it involves mutual love, respect and sharing.

It must be admitted that this dynamic view of mission has sometimes been replaced by a much more static and institutionalized concept. The result has been that the limited objectives of apostolic missions have been expanded to include goals which have required repeated postponement of the termination of the mission. At the home end, British Christians have come to regard 'the mission' as a permanent institution, and thus they are saddened by events in Africa or Asia which would have called forth apostolic hallelujahs!

Part of our task today, then, involves a process of education by means of which Christians in the West will become aware of contemporary realities in relation to the many burgeoning young churches in lands in Africa, Asia and South America which have been traditionally regarded as 'the mission fields'. What is actually occurring at present as a direct outcome of missionary labours over the past two centuries is that there is an unmistakable shift in the spiritual and theological centre of gravity away from the older churches of Europe and North America and towards the vibrant young churches of the Third World. As nations like Britain and Holland become spiritual wastelands (of which more later), new centres of vitality and importance in church growth and theological construction are emerging in Asia, Africa and Latin America — where the majority of Christians will be living in the year 2000.

In view of this, we must surely be able to say, with profound thankfulness, that in relation to much of the dedicated and sacrificial labours of generations of missionaries in the past two hundred years, *mission has been accomplished*. The extent to which we are able to recognize the areas in which this is the case may determine our ability to face up to the new missionary challenges of our own age.

Where other gods hold sway.

When William Carey and John Thomas set sail for India on 13 June 1793, they did so with great hopes of reaping an abundant spiritual harvest among the peoples of that subcontinent. They knew that the Hindu caste system would present problems when it

154

came to forming an indigenous church in India, but they were sure that such difficulties would be surmounted and that the kingdom of Christ would come in great power among Hindus. This confidence was related to the eschatological beliefs which played a central part in the emergence of modern missions: Carey and all his brethren had caught Jonathan Edwards's thrilling conviction that the age of millennial glory might be about to burst forth. At the end of the eighteenth century, evangelicals were agreed on the subject of eschatology. Whatever other differences they might have had, they believed that they could discern what William Williams called the breaking of the dawn of a 'blessed jubilee' above 'the gloomy hills of darkness'. We surely cannot fault these men for their confidence that the saving purposes of God must include the display of divine grace among the millions of people devoted to non-Christian faiths. Carey shared Paul's conviction that those who had not yet been told about Christ would come to understand, and he related this to India's teeming millions, Hindus and Muslims.

Resistance to the gospel

Alas, the task proved to be much more difficult than had been anticipated. The age of millennial glory did not come, and the ancient walls of Hinduism failed to crumble and collapse at the sound of the gospel trumpets. Faced with the reality of the situation in India, Carey came to believe that his task was to act as a pioneer, breaking the ground and preparing the way 'for more successful missionaries'. Some of his colleagues gave frank expression to their feelings of spiritual anguish at the apparent failure of the gospel to make significant inroads into the Hindu strongholds. William Ward wrote to an American correspondent in 1821 that the 'restricted progress of Christianity and the moral darkness in which so great a part of the globe has remained, notwithstanding the Sun of Righteousness has arisen . . . forms one of the most mysterious dispensations of Providence which has ever occupied human attention'. Here is a man who, from first-hand experience of Hinduism and Islam, is wrestling with the profound problem of the unevangelized millions.

Resurgence of other religions

I would suggest that if we do not share something of Ward's anguish and perplexity it can only be because we have failed to grasp the facts concerning the religions of the world at the close of the twentieth century. If Carey and Ward were distressed by the knowledge that Hinduism and Islam often appeared to be impervious to the power of the gospel, what should we feel today as, two hundred years later, we witness the resurgence and advance of these religions in many parts of the earth? According to Barrett there are over 817 million Muslims in the world and, given present rates of growth, this figure will rise to over 1,200 million by the end of the century. Words written by Hendrik Kraemer concerning the non-Christian religions seem as relevant now as when they were published in 1956: 'A century ago we could ignore their existence. They seemed immaterial to the dominating curve of history so patently embodied in the Western world. Today it is impossible to ignore them; and their development, good or evil, will affect all other parts of the world.'[2]

Some readers may ask how these facts can be related to those mentioned previously concerning the phenomenal growth of the church in the Third World. The answer is that such growth has occurred mainly in areas in which primal, or traditional, religions predominated; only very rarely have Christian missions experienced marked success where one of the so-called world religions holds sway. Thus, the problem of the great religions remains somewhere near the top of the missionary agenda of the contemporary church; we simply cannot evade the question, 'How shall *they* hear?'

The collapse of Christendom

There is another totally new factor in our situation today which contrasts dramatically with the age of William Carey. At the end of the eighteenth century, Hindus and Muslims were 'Far, far away . . .' This is no longer the case: Christendom has collapsed; the East has moved west, and the once distant and unknown heathen has become the pleasant Pakistani Muslim who runs the local newsagent's shop. It is absolutely essential to our understanding of mission today that we grasp the full implications of the multi-faith and multicultural character of our own society. It is estimated that there are approximately 1.2 million Muslims resident within the United Kingdom. So far as eastern religions are concerned, an even more amazing reversal has occurred. Contrary to Kipling's oft-quoted lines, the East and West *have* met, and Hindu and Buddhist religious philosophies are among the many world views on offer in our pluralistic society. It is possible to study the Hindu Vedas in an Ashram in a Buckinghamshire village, or to join Buddhist study groups from Aberdeen to Penzance.

What does all this mean in relation to Christian mission? Our belief in divine providence surely leads us to conclude that the unprecedented movement of peoples in the modern era, together with the astonishing traffic in religious ideas, must be the harbinger of new things in the earth. The breaking down of cultural barriers and the growth of pluralism are likely to open new doors of opportunity for witness to peoples of other faiths. Moreover, as these religions confront 'modernity' and are themselves compelled to face the challenges of the pluralistic and secularist spirit of the contemporary world, it is likely that quite new openings for Christian testimony will arise. Not that such testimony will be an easy thing. British Christians are likely to discover what missionaries in Africa and India already know: that witness to Hindus or Muslims can only succeed within the context of a living demonstration of the love and grace of Christ in the life of the believer, and that it demands careful thought and serious theological reflection. In other words, we will need to take very seriously the problem of the *cross-cultural* communication of the gospel.

Let me quote, by way of example, from a thesis written by a Nigerian student who came from an area in which Christians and Muslims lived as neighbours in the same villages. The thesis was entitled *The Communication of the Christian Faith to Muslims: A New Approach*. In the introduction the writer confessed: 'If ever I made any attempt to approach a Muslim, it was in a spirit of confrontation which led to conflict and we parted. No fruit has ever come of it in any way.' Alas, this testimony may be regarded as a microcosm of Christian-Muslim contact over the centuries. May we not hope that with the demise of Christendom (the religio-political system which launched the Crusades against Islam) and the surfacing of deep questions from within these religions, Christians may be granted the opportunity of a 'new approach' to the non-Christian peoples of the world?

Mission and the Communist lands

We noted earlier the tremendous increase in the numbers of people who belong within the categories of 'non-religious' or 'atheist'. On the basis of present trends, it is estimated that over 1,334 million people will belong within these groups by the end of the century. This figure includes both the large number of people in the Western world who are unable to affirm belief in God, and also the millions of non-religious people living in lands where rejection of religion is official state policy. We shall return to the former in a moment, but first of all let us consider Christian mission in Communist lands.

Here the confusion to which reference was made at the beginning of this chapter becomes acute. The widening socio-political chasm between East and West appears to make 'missions' to Communist lands impossible. The Iron Curtain, which is all too clearly given objective physical expression in the Berlin Wall, leaves us with a feeling of impotence and frustration. What can we do?

Maintaining a Christian world view

First, I suggest that we strive to maintain a biblical and Christian view of the world and its peoples. In an age when millions of men living under a different socio-political system from our own are constantly and publicly stereotyped in terms of images and labels derived from a secular political ideology, this is no easy thing to do. The Russian nation is depicted as a rapacious bear; Russians are described in collectivist and depersonalized language as 'Reds' or 'Commies'. In this process, millions of people living in Eastern Europe cease to be thought of as those who share with us a common humanity derived from the one Creator; instead they become hated symbols. Without making any specific political judgment, we must surely insist that such categorization is sinful; it violates fundamental biblical principles concerning the unity of mankind and runs directly counter to the incarnate example of Christ. Jesus quite specifically repudiated the racial and ideological stereotypes embedded within Jewish social thought at the time of His ministry. Displaying the liberating power of the kingdom, He burst through such divisive attitudes, challenging the conventions of His age and shocking even His closest followers by the freedom with which, for example, He spoke with a Samaritan woman. Christians who recognize the authority of Jesus Christ as Lord, and who seek to obey His command to 'make disciples of *all* nations', will repudiate the rhetoric of cold war, and also the philosophy, or world view, which gave birth to it. Our vision is a much wider one. Like Paul, we 'regard no one from a worldly point of view' (2 Cor. 5:16) and believe that the reconciling message of the gospel, which in ancient times destroyed the 'dividing wall of hostility' between Jews and Gentiles (Eph. 2:14), will yet cause the removal of Iron Curtains and demonstrate afresh its power to 'heal the nations'.

Understanding other beliefs

Second, it is a fundamental missiological principle that Christ's evangelists must, by the use of all possible means, seek to *understand* the beliefs of those to whom they desire to communicate the message of the gospel. Whether those to whom we communicate are Muslims, Hindus or Marxists, their religion or ideology must be taken seriously. This will involve a readiness on our part to speak with such people, entering into serious conversation in order to discover exactly what they believe and why they believe as they do. As far as Communism is concerned, a knowledge of the historical factors involved in the Marxist rejection of religion is vital. Just as Muhammed cannot be understood apart from his encounter with a corrupt form of Christianity in Arabia, so the attitude of the Soviet Union towards religion must be seen within the context of Russian history in the nineteenth century and, in particular, the callous indifference of the Orthodox Church to appalling social and political injustice. Mission to the Communist world will demand of Christians that they take the Marxist critique of religion very seriously and are able to demonstrate irrefutable evidence that faith in Christ produces lives which are not susceptible to such a critique. Milan Machovec, the Czechoslovak Marxist philosopher, writes that 'Sunday or conventional or fellow-travelling Christians' do nothing to compel Marxists to re-evaluate their ideological stance on religion, but he testifies that the encounter with genuine believers

> could create a situation in which Marxists had to start thinking about religion in a more subtle way; for only such deeply Christian spirits could not be denounced, even by the strictest 'guardians of Marxist orthodoxy', as mere pawns of capitalism or as dispensers of opium to the people. They almost compelled Marxist thinkers to re-examine certain traditional Christian positions, and they achieved this not through harshness but through openness and love.[3]

Believing in the power of God

Thirdly, if, for the present, contacts between East and West are limited, we are called to the exercise of faith and prayer, and to a sensitive awareness of what God may be doing in Communist lands *without our aid*. Alexander Solzhenitsyn has testified that it was in a Siberian prison camp that he first understood reality: 'It was there that I realised that the line between good and evil passes not between countries, not between political parties, but down, straight down, each separate individual human heart.'

Perhaps of all the signs of the times today none is more significant, more pregnant with meaning for the future of our world, than recent events in China. In 1980 the *World Christian Encyclopedia* estimated the number of baptized members of known churches in China at 1,800,000. It is now evident that this figure was far too low and the burgeoning house-church movement in China may number as many as 98 million members! Given such a dynamic rate of growth, it is likely that East Asia will become the 'major Christian global power-house of the twenty-first century'. After reminding us that this astonishing development has occurred with little or no active help from Western Christianity, except prayer, Barrett asks, 'What totally new surprises of this type, completely unknown and unexpected, can God have in store for the world of the twenty-first century?'[4]

Back to Jerusalem: re-evangelizing the post-Christian West

We spoke earlier of an outdated concept of mission in which evangelization is thought of as occurring 'Far, far away . . .' Such a view rested upon the double assumption that the heathen were to be found in distant places and that 'we' are all Christians; mission was based in a Christian country. Clearly, both these assumptions are now untenable. Yet how far do British Christians recognize that in respect of their own culture they are today in a totally missionary situation? And to what extent do they appreciate that this means living and witnessing in an alien environment and being compelled to offer some fairly radical challenges to the fundamental assumptions of that culture? To judge from the findings of modern sociologists, not too many Christians are troubled by such questions. In the post-Christian world, we are told, religion has retreated to the periphery of society; it has become a personal and private matter. Thus the sociologist of religion, Bryan Wilson, commenting on the growth of new cults, argues that, far from representing a revival of religion in secular society, they have 'no real consequence for other social institutions, for political power structures, for technological constraints and controls. They add nothing to any prospective reintegration of society, and contribute nothing towards the culture by which a society might live.'[5] In so far as it is concerned almost exclusively with personal religion, these words offer a challenge to a great deal which today passes under the name of evangelical Christianity. Certainly, of all the missiological tasks facing the churches of the West, none is of greater importance and urgency than the re-evangelization of our own culture; the proclamation in the midst of secular society that Jesus Christ is LORD.

A new opportunity.

In considering this aspect of mission two points need to be remembered. First, there is growing evidence of a profound social and cultural crisis within the Western world which creates a tremendous opportunity for Christian mission. The decline of the power of religion in the West has long been recognized; but what is so significant today is the fact that secular humanism, the tradition stemming from the Enlightenment which was supposed to replace religion and render it unnecessary, is itself in the throes of deep and terminal sickness. These words are being typed on the morning after the sickening events in Brussels, in which over forty people

160

have died at a football match. Such events compel deep questioning concerning the state of our society by people who, not long ago, were satisfied with a fully secular world view. Take this sentence from Bryan Wilson:

> The erosion of the traditional culture of western society has been in process, unevenly and spasmodically, for a considerable time. We have been learning or half-learning how to live without a culture, or with the rags and tatters of an earlier culture still clutched about the parts of us that we least care to expose.[6]

Can we read such words without hearing the voice of Him who says, 'See, I have placed before you an open door . . .'?

The need for a virile message

Secondly, if we are to go through that door, we must do so with a message which offers secular man something *more than* a personal spiritual salvation which satisfies his individual need but allows him to go on living in a state of peaceful coexistence with a godless culture. This sort of Christianity departs in the most radical way from the biblical gospel, withdrawing into an area of privatized religion and accepting the status of a religious cult. Indeed, by relieving the anxieties of people who must live in secular society *without* challenging the fundamental assumptions of that society, it sails very close to the Marxist accusation of being nothing more than 'opium for the people'. The early church, at the cost of immense suffering, refused to accept such a role in pagan society. Rome could easily have accommodated one more religious sect, but Christians refused to be type-cast in this way, and went on insisting that the authority of their Redeemer could not be limited to a conveniently compartmentalized sphere of life where it offered no challenge to the prevailing consensus.

It seems to me that Christians today face an analogous situation: modern secular culture stemming from the Enlightenment represented an attempt to return to pre-Christian values, to build society on a basis from which the authority of Christ was quite deliberately excluded. The realization of this fact has enormous implications touching every aspect of life, from social ethics to economics and politics. So far as the Christian mission in the Western world is concerned, we are surely called to repent of the extent to which we have allowed the gospel message to be muted by a syncretistic alliance with post-Enlightenment culture.

PREPARING THE CHURCH FOR MISSION
IN THE MODERN WORLD

I have concentrated on the overall picture and have tried to give a global survey of the state of mission in the modern world. In this final section I would like to offer some practical suggestions as to how the church may be prepared for the task of bearing witness to Christ at the close of the twentieth century.

The whole gospel for the whole man

The question of the relationship between preaching and social activity has been a burning issue in much contemporary missiology. No one, I imagine, could fail to rejoice in the rediscovery of the evangelical social conscience, but there remains considerable uncertainty as to just how such concerns are to be integrated within a biblical pattern of witness. Those of us who are acquainted with leprosy hospitals in Africa, where the love of Christ is declared by word and deed to people afflicted with a disease which brings both physical suffering and social stigma, may perhaps be forgiven for wondering what the problem is. Could it be that at the root of our difficulties is an unbiblical, or at least sub-biblical, view of the gospel? Where in the Bible can we find a divorce between word and deed, proclamation and practice? Everywhere in Scripture, from the Old Testament prophets to the life and teaching of Jesus and the apostolic writings, a holistic view of truth prevails: word and deed belong together as the two witnesses to the reality of the kingdom of God. Even in the Pastoral Epistles, in which the stress upon orthodoxy is strong, we find Paul saying that 'slave traders and liars and perjurers' are 'contrary to the sound doctrine that conforms to the glorious gospel' (1 Tim. 1:10). Thus, sound doctrine is not merely a matter of right belief; the good news of the gospel relates to man *as man*, and not just some spiritual part of him abstracted from his historical existence. The New Testament seems unaware of our problem here; it everywhere insists that in any authentic witness to the gospel word and deed are interrelated.

The recognition of the holistic character of the Christian mission enables us to understand how the entire church, rather than just a minority of its members who possess particular gifts, is called to mission. Of course, gifts of preaching, evangelism and church-planting are of paramount importance, and every church should pray earnestly for the appearance of such gifts in their midst. But these are not the only gifts which Christ uses within

162

the context of mission — whether in Lagos, Hong Kong, Lima, or in the Rhondda Valley. No disciple of Jesus can evade the call to mission: the medical doctor, the engineer, the economist, the wife and mother — *all* are called to bear witness to Christ by word of mouth and through deeds of kindness and mercy which commend the gospel.

Preparation for cross-cultural communication

Earlier in this chapter I suggested that the 'problem' of the great world religions and the unevangelized millions must lie near the top of the churches' agenda. How can we face this issue? Clearly there are places where regular social contact between Christians and adherents of these faiths makes meaningful conversation possible. Even in some closed countries a 'tent-making' ministry is feasible, and quietly and discreetly a witness to Christ is being borne. Even where such openings do not exist, the thirst for Western technology gives access to businessmen and others. A knowledge of church history will prevent us from under-estimating the missionary potential of such contacts. And in lands where open verbal testimony is forbidden let us never overlook the power of a genuinely Christlike *life*. Perhaps there are situations where an imposed silence may not be an altogether bad thing, where — as in Hindu Nepal, for instance — open preaching is forbidden, and yet the church is growing as a direct consequence of the witness to Christ in the beauty of the lives of His people. Hindus have often complained that Christians 'talk too much', and that the Christ who had nowhere to lay His head has been hidden from view by 'the imagined Jesus pictured to them by the so-called Christian countries'.[7] The words of Norman Anderson concerning Islam might equally apply to witness to Hindus or Buddhists or, for that matter, to Marxists: 'We have yet to see what would happen if the gospel of the living Christ *were adequately presented* to the hundreds of millions of men and women who make up the world of Islam' (italics mine).[8]

Now, of all the places where an 'adequate presentation' of the gospel to Muslims and Hindus is possible, none should be of greater concern to British Christians than that which exists on their own doorsteps, so to speak. The greatest missionary openings today are to be found not in Saudi-Arabia or Pakistan, but in the multicultural cities of London, Birmingham and Brad-ford. Yet, while providence has brought the 'mission field' to our doorsteps in terms of geographical proximity, most evangelical churches remain separated from the ethnic minority communities by a veritable chasm of socio-cultural distance and misunderstanding. Old attitudes die hard, as I discovered recently when a church choir at a missionary weekend rose and sang:

Far, far away in heathen darkness dwelling,
Millions of souls for ever may be lost.

We may smile at this. Yet all too often our attitudes and, indeed, the patterns of evangelism, education and missionary activity seen in our churches betray a mentality which may have been relevant to the nineteenth century but is sadly out of touch with contemporary realities. I suggest that we need something approaching a revolutionary change of attitude. The mind-set associated with Christendom clings to us in all sorts of subtle ways, and it is inimical to the fulfilling of our missionary calling in a situation not unlike that which faced the apostles at the beginning of Christian history.

Given this context, a whole string of important questions clamour for attention. How can our congregations become the instruments of mission within the pluralistic and multicultural society of modern Britain? How can biblical principles of cross-cultural communication be taught, in order that real lines of conversation may be opened between believers and non-Christians in our society? And how long can we tolerate a situation in which men are prepared for pastoral ministry in a multi-faith society with little or no training in missiology? This last question is crucial, since congregations can hardly be blamed for failure in mission if their leaders have not grasped the real nature of the task confronting the people of God today.

The indispensable prerequisites: hope and prayer

The importance of a biblical theology of hope in relation to the origins of the modern missionary movement can be seen in Iain Murray's excellent book *The Puritan Hope*. Alas, such hope is in short supply today. Too many Christians base their view of the future either upon secular prognostications related to 'current trends', or upon a misreading of biblical prophecy in which the glorious vistas of the promises of God are lost from view. In the story of Scott's Antarctic journey there is a point at which atmospheric conditions led to snow and sky merging into a single white blank, with nothing on which the eye could fix to give direction. Before long they discovered that they were coming back on their own tracks! Is not this a picture of much modern Christianity: going round in circles in a world without horizons? We need renewed confidence in God and in His promises, judging the prospects for mission not on the basis of the current state of the world but in relation to faith in a sovereign Lord who is able, even in the midst of a new cold war, to do 'immeasurably more than all we ask or imagine' (Eph. 3:20).

Finally, the modern missionary movement was preceded both by a recovery of a biblically based hope and also by a tremendous upsurge in united evangelical praying. John Sutcliff of Olney republished Jonathan Edwards's *Humble Attempt*[9] in 1789, and called for the establishment of groups to pray for revival all across Britain, 'offering up their united prayers, like so many clouds of incense before the Most High'. Perhaps Carey's words, uttered amid the flood-tide of Enlightenment humanism, can inspire us anew at the close of the twentieth century, when that tide has long since turned, leaving Western man alone on a desolate cultural wasteland: 'Expect great things from God; attempt great things for God.'

NOTES

1 David Barrett, 'Annual Statistical Table on Global Mission', *International Bulletin of Missionary Research,* 9.1 (1985), pp.30-31.
2 Hendrik Kraemer, *Religion and the Christian Faith* (Lutterworth, 1956), p.23.
3 Milan Machovec, *A Marxist Looks at Jesus* (Darton, Longman & Todd, 1976), p.96.
4 David Barrett, 'Annual Statistical Table'.
5 Bryan Wilson, *Contemporary Transformations of Religion* (Clarendon, 1979), p.96.
6 Bryan Wilson, p.112.
7 See Raymond Windsor in *We Believe in Mission*, ed. by John Wallis (Marshalls/STL, 1983), p.89.
8 J.N.D. Anderson, *The World's Religions* (Inter-Varsity Press, 1975), p.134.
9 Jonathan Edwards, 'An Humble Attempt to Promote Explicit Agreement and Visible Union of God's People, in Extraordinary Prayer, for the Revival of Religion and the Advancement of Christ's Kingdom on Earth', in *Works* (Banner of Truth, 1974), vol.2, pp.278-312.

QUESTIONS FOR DISCUSSION

a) According to this chapter, 'our attitudes . . . patterns of evangelism, education and missionary activity . . . betray a mentality which may have been relevant to the nineteenth century but is sadly out of touch with contemporary realities'. How far do you agree with this? and in what ways should our attitudes and practices be changed to meet the challenge of mission today?

b)What *are* the 'fundamental assumptions' of Western society and culture which run counter to the gospel, and how can Christians develop and maintain patterns of life, corporate as well as individual, which provide an alternative vision of human existence based on the gospel? Consider Matthew 6:19-34; Ephesians 4:17-24; 1 John 2:15-17.

c) In advance of a meeting, members of the group can be asked to discover all they can about one specific non-Christian belief-system (Islam, Buddhism, Hinduism, Marxism — or some local sect or new religious movement), and then share this information with the whole group. Try, as it were, to understand the belief-system from the *inside*, focusing upon what adherents would see as its strong points, not discussing it because of what you perceive to be its obvious errors. Then, discuss how the message of Christ might be presented effectively to people holding each of these particular world-views. Consider Acts 15:12-21 (noting especially how the Council in Jerusalem refused to impose Jewish culture on Gentile converts); 1 Corinthians 9:19-23; Galatians 2:11-16.

FURTHER READING

J.H. Bavinck's *An Introduction to the Science of Missions* (Presbyterian & Reformed, 1960) is old but still unsurpassed as a general introduction to missiology. *The World's Religions* (Lion Publishing, 1982) should be in every church library. On Marxism and Christianity Klaus Bockmuehl's *The Challenge of Marxism* (Inter-Varsity Press, 1980) is excellent, while J.A. Walter has attempted to address modern secularists in his *A Long Way From Home* (Paternoster, 1979). Lesslie Newbigin is not a conservative evangelical, but his books *The Other Side of 1984* (World Council of Churches, 1983) and *Foolishness To The Greeks* (World Council of Churches, 1986) are well worth reading. On the application of modern principles of communication to mission the various works of Eugene Nida are helpful, especially *Message and Mission* (William Carey Library, 1960). Finally, a very useful warning as to the problems and pitfalls in cross-cultural communication will be found in Rhena Taylor's *Rough Edges* (Inter-Varsity Press, 1979).

BIBLIOGRAPHY

A. BOOKS

Action on Unemployment (Church Action with the Unemployed, 1984).

J. N. D. Anderson, *The World's Religions* (Inter-Varsity Press, 1975).

Archbishop of Canterbury's Commission on Urban Priority Areas, *Faith in the City: A Call for Action by Church and Nation* (Church House Publishing, 1985).

A. Atkins, *Split Image* (Hodder & Stoughton, 1987).

J. Baldwin, 'Women's Ministry — A New Look at the Biblical Texts', in *The Role of Women,* ed. by S. Lees (Inter-Varsity Press 1984), pp.158-76.

O. R. Barclay, 'The Nature of Christian Morality', in *Law, Morality and the Bible,* ed. by B. N. Kaye and G. J. Wenham (Inter-Varsity Press, 1978), pp.125-50.

O. R. Barclay, *Developing a Christian Mind* (Inter-Varsity Press, 1984).

J. H. Bavinck, *An Introduction to the Science of Missions* (Presbyterian & Reformed, 1960).

J. Benington, *Culture, Class and Christian Beliefs* (Scripture Union, 1973).

K. Bockmuehl, *The Challenge of Marxism* (Inter-Varsity Press, 1980).

E. Braund, *The Young Woman Who Lived in a Shoe* (Prisca, 1984).

S. S. Brown, *Thomas Chalmers and the Godly Commonwealth* (Oxford University Press, 1982).

E. Brunner, *Christianity and Civilisation,* 2 vols (Nisbet, 1947-8).

J. Calvin, *Institutes of the Christian Religion* (James Clarke, 1962).

H. F. R. Catherwood, *The Christian in Industrial Society* (Tyndale Press, 1966).

H. F. R. Catherwood, *The Christian Citizen* (Hodder & Stoughton, 1969).

H. F. R. Catherwood, *A Better Way* (Inter-Varsity Press, 1975).

The Christian and the State in Revolutionary Times (Westminster Conference, 1975).

L. J. Coppes, *Who Will Lead Us?* (Pilgrim Publishing House, 1977).

A. Dallimore, *Spurgeon: A New Biography* (Banner of Truth, 1985).

G. W. Davies, *The Christian, the Church and Daily Work* (Evangelical Press of Wales, 1984).

J. Edwards, 'Christian Charity', in *Works* (Banner of Truth, 1974), vol.2, pp.163-73.

Evangelism and Social Responsibility (Lausanne Conference Report — Paternoster, 1982).

M. J. Evans, *Woman in the Bible* (Paternoster, 1983).

D. Field, 'Headship in Marriage: The Husband's View', in *The Role of Women*, ed. by S. Lees (Inter-Varsity Press, 1984), pp.43-63.

J. K. Galbraith, *The Anatomy of Power* (Corgi Books, 1983).

N. Geisler, *Options in Contemporary Christian Ethics* (Baker, 1981).

W. Green, *The Christian and Unemployment* (Mowbray, 1982).

R. S. Greenway, *Discipling the City* (Baker, 1979).

B. Griffiths, *The Creation of Wealth* (Hodder & Stoughton, 1984).

C. Handy, *The Future of Work* (Blackwell, 1984).

W. Hendriksen, *Timothy and Titus* (Banner of Truth, 1964).

C. F. H. Henry, *Aspects of Christian Social Ethics* (Eerdmans, 1964).

B. V. Hill, *Faith at the Blackboard* (Eerdmans, 1982).

C. Hodge, *1 Corinthians* (Banner of Truth, 1974).

F. Hughes, *Whose Child?* (Association of Christian Teachers of Wales, 1982).

J. Hurley, *Man and Woman in Biblical Perspective* (Inter-Varsity Press, 1981).

R. Joslin, *Urban Harvest* (Evangelical Press, 1982).

B. N. Kaye, *Using the Bible in Ethics* (Grove Books, 1976).

B. N. Kaye and G. J. Wenham (ed.), *Law, Morality and the Bible* (Inter-Varsity Press, 1978).

D. Kidner, *The Message of Hosea* (Inter-Varsity Press, 1981).

H. Kraemer, *Religion and the Christian Faith* (Lutterworth, 1956).

A. Kuyper, *Lectures on Calvinism* (Eerdmans, n.d.).

M. S. Langley, *Equal Woman* (Marshalls, 1983).

S. Lees (ed.), *The Role of Women* (Inter-Varsity Press, 1984).

R. C. H. Lenski, *Interpretation of St Paul's Epistles: Colossians-*

Philemon (Wartburg Press, n.d.).

D. M. Lloyd-Jones, *Studies in the Sermon on the Mount* (Inter-Varsity Press, 1959).

D. M. Lloyd-Jones, *Life in the Spirit* (Banner of Truth, 1974).

D. M. Lloyd-Jones, *The Doctor Himself* (Christian Medical Fellowship, 1982).

D. Lyon, *The Steeple's Shadow* (SPCK, 1985).

M. Machovec, *A Marxist Looks at Jesus* (Darton, Longman & Todd, 1976).

J. MacMurray, *Freedom in the Modern World* (Faber, 1968).

I. H. Marshall, 'Using the Bible in Ethics', in *Essays in Evangelical Social Ethics,* ed. by D. F. Wright (Paternoster, n.d.), pp.39-55.

I. H. Marshall, 'The Role of Women in the Church', in *The Role of Women,* ed. by S. Lees (Inter-Varsity Press, 1984), pp.177-97.

C. Martin, *You've Got to Start Somewhere When You Think About Education* (Inter-Varsity Press, 1979).

C. Martin, *Have Schools Lost Their Way?* (Grove Books, 1980).

P. May, *Which Way to School?* (Lion Publishing, 1972).

P. May, *Which Way to Teach?* (Inter-Varsity Press, 1981).

J. A. Motyer, *The Message of Amos* (Inter-Varsity Press, 1974).

J. A. Motyer, *The Message of James* (Inter-Varsity Press, 1985).

I. H. Murray, *D. Martyn Lloyd-Jones, The First Forty Years* (Banner of Truth, 1982).

J. Murray, 'The Finality and Sufficiency of Scripture', in *Collected Writings, I: The Claims of Truth* (Banner of Truth, 1976), pp.16-22.

L. Newbigin, *The Other Side of 1984* (World Council of Churches, 1983).

L. Newbigin, *Foolishness to the Greeks* (World Council of Churches, 1986).

E. Nida, *Message and Mission* (William Carey Library, 1960).

R. Niebuhr, *Moral Man and Immoral Society* (Scribner, 1960).

S. Olyott, 'Fostering and Adoption', in *Christian Family Matters,* ed. by I. Shaw (Evangelical Press of Wales, 1985), pp.81-92.

J. I. Packer, 'Conscience, Choice and Character', in *Law, Morality and the Bible,* ed. by B. N. Kaye and G. J. Wenham (Inter-Varsity Press, 1978), pp.168-92.

J. I. Packer, 'Why Preach?', in *Preaching,* ed. by S. T. Logan (Evangelical Press, 1986), pp.1-29.

G. Pearson, *Hooligan* (Macmillan, 1983).

M. L. Peterson, *Philosophy of Education: Issues and Options* (Inter-Varsity Press, 1987).

D. Potter, 'The Handicapped Child', in *Christian Family Matters,* ed. by I. Shaw (Evangelical Press of Wales, 1985), pp.71-9.

D. Prior, *The Message of 1 Corinthians* (Inter-Varsity Press, 1985).

J. R. Richards, *The Sceptical Feminist* (Penguin Books, 1982).

R. J. Rushdoony, *Bread Upon the Waters* (Cornerstone Publishers, 1974).

R. J. Rushdoony, *Institutes of Biblical Law* (Presbyterian & Reformed, 1973).

S. Rutherford, *Lex Rex: or, The Law and the Prince (c.1644)*, contained in *The Presbyterian's Armoury* (Robert Ogle and Oliver & Boyd, 1843), vol. 3.

F. A. Schaeffer, *A Christian Manifesto* (Pickering & Inglis, 1982).

F. A. Schaeffer, *The Church at the End of the Twentieth Century* (Hodder & Stoughton, 1975).

M. Schluter and R. Clements, *Reactivating the Extended Family: From Biblical Norms to Public Policy in Britain* (Jubilee Centre, 1986).

R. Smith, *Unemployment and Health* (Oxford University Press, 1987).

N. Stonehouse, *The Witness of Matthew and Mark to Christ* (Baker, 1979).

A. Storkey, *A Christian Social Perspective* (Inter-Varsity Press, 1979).

E. Storkey, *What's Right With Feminism?* (SPCK, 1985).

J. Stott, *The Message of the Sermon on the Mount* (Inter-Varsity Press, 1978).

J. Stott, *The Message of Ephesians* (Inter-Varsity Press, 1979).

J. Stott, *Issues Facing Christians Today* (Marshalls, 1984).

R. Taylor, *Rough Edges* (Inter-Varsity Press, 1979).

P. Thompson, *To the Heart of the City* (Hodder & Stoughton, n.d.).

A. N. Triton, *Salt to the World: The Christian and Social Involvement* (Inter-Varsity Press, 1978).

J. Wallis, *The New Radical* (Lion Publishing, 1983).

J. Wallis, *We Believe in Mission* (Marshalls/STL, 1983).

J. A. Walter, *A Long Way From Home* (Paternoster, 1979).

J. A. Walter, *Fair Shares* (Handsel Press, 1985).

C. P. Warren, *Comprehensive Education* (Paternoster Press, 1979).

H. Wilmer, 'Towards a Theology of the State', in *Essays in Evangelical Social Ethics* ed. by D. F. Wright (Paternoster, n.d.), pp.85-102.

B. Wilson, *Contemporary Transformations of Religion* (Clarendon Press, 1979).

D. J. Winwood, *Ways to Work With the Young Unemployed*

(Methodist Association of Youth Clubs, 1981).

World's Religions, The (Lion Publishing, 1982).

C. J. H. Wright, *Living as the People of God* (Inter-Varsity Press, 1983).

D. F. Wright (ed.), *Essays in Evangelical Social Ethics* (Paternoster, n.d.).

P. Y. de Yong, *The Ministry of Mercy for Today* (Baker, 1952).

B. ARTICLES

D. Barrett, 'Annual Statistical Table on Global Mission', *International Bulletin of Missionary Research*, 9 (January 1985), pp.30-31.

D. Field, 'Rights and Responsibilities: Are They in Conflict?', *Christian Arena*, 37.4 (December 1984), pp.9-15.

D. Freeman, 'Sabbatical Year', in *Illustrated Bible Dictionary* ed. by J. D. Douglas (Inter-Varsity Press, 1980).

F. Hughes, 'The Aims of Education', *Spectrum*, 15.3 (1983), pp.7-11.

D. MacLeod, 'The Basis of Christian Unity', *Evangel*, 3.3 (1985), pp.2-11.

M. Manton, 'The Role of Women in the Church', *Evangelical Magazine of Wales*, 20.3 (1981), pp.10-11.

M. Manton, 'Teach Me Thy Way', *Evangelical Magazine of Wales*, 20.4 (1981), pp.8-11.

M. E. Marty, 'Social Service: Godly and Godless', *Social Service Review*, 54 (1980), pp.463-81.

D. Smith, 'The Bible and Culture', *Christian Arena*, 39.4 (1986), pp.5-8.

A. F. Walls, 'Deacon' in *New Bible Dictionary*, ed. by J. D. Douglas (Inter-Varsity Press, 1962).

C. AUDIO TAPES

D. Zink, *Interpreting the 'Culturally Relative' in Scripture* (L'Abri Fellowship, 1986 — 49 Lynbrook Road, Southborough, MA 01772, USA).

Index of Scripture References

Genesis
1:26-31   97, 109
1:27   124
2:9   63
2:18   125
3:12   12
3:17   97
4:1-16   12
4:9   12
5:1,3   139
9:6   109
12:1   30
20:8-10   44
21:8-14   15, 16
22   15

Exodus
1:15-22   16
22:26-27   63f.
23:9   135, 140

Leviticus
19   135
19:18   110
19:34   140
25:2-4   94
25:8   95

Numbers
11:5   19
13:28-33   78

Deuteronomy
5:12-15   94
6:5   110
6:6ff.   110, 112
6:12   94
8:11ff.   94
10:18-19   135, 140
15:7-18   135
15:10   141, 147

15:11   142, 147, 149
17:14ff.   69
24:1-4   28, 139
24:18   140

Joshua
2:4-5   16
5:13   78
5:15   79
6:3   79
6:16   79
23:15-16   95

Judges
4:9   125

1 Samuel
8:15,17   26
15:23   69

Ezra
9   16
10   16
10:9ff.   15, 139

Nehemiah
8—10   20

Job
31:13-15   138

Psalms
72:4   72
139   70

Proverbs
3:27-28   147
11:24-25   141
14:31   138
17:5   138
19:17   138

22:2   138
28:27   141
31   122, 131

Ecclesiastes
2:10-11   98
7:10   19

Isaiah
1:16-17   135
1:18-20   42
13—24   138
32:15-20   45
35:5-6   135
42:18-19   135
43:8   135
58:10   147

Jeremiah
46—51   138

Ezekiel
25—32   138

Daniel
1:8ff.   70
3   15, 16
6   15, 16

Hosea
2:19   14

Amos
1:1—2:5   138
5:21-24   14, 135
8:4ff.   95

Zephaniah
2   138

Zechariah
12:12-14   12

Matthew
5   11, 28, 40
5—7   27
5:13-16   42, 69,
             135, 149
5:17   27f.
5:22   20
5:32   43
5:39   66
5:44-48   41, 46,
             135, 138, 144
6:1-15   141, 149
6:3   147
6:10   53
6:19-34   166
7:6   115
7:9-11   138
7:12   25
10:42   141
12:1-8   16
12:32   20
15:14   135
15:32   41
19:1-10   28, 139
19:8   27, 42, 64
19:9   43
19:12   130
20:25-28   110
22:21   68
22:37-40   15, 110
23:14   68
23:23   20
25:31-46   146, 149
28:19   158

Mark
1:38   89
6:30-44   149
6:37   141
7:11   49
10:41-45   149
12:37   80
14:7   142
14:3-11   149
16:15   80

Luke
1:52-53   145
4:18   72, 145
6:20-36   145
6:32-34   138
6:35   145
6:36   139
7:22   145

10:1   82
10:30-37   102, 144
12:15   110
12:16-21   98
12:35-38   149
12:48   28
13:32   68
14:7   142
14:13-14   141
14:18,21   84
15:4   84
16:1-12   98
22:25-27   146, 149

John
5:30   125
6:26-27   142, 149
9:39   135
13:1-17   146, 149
15:19   138
17:11   8
17:14   8
19:11   20

Acts
1:14   125
2:17-18   129
2:44-47   99
4:32-35   99, 135,
             147
6:1-2   49
6:1-6   99, 142,
             145, 149
9:6   89
9:36   125, 140
10:34   80
10:38   140
12:12   125
14:26   153
15:12-21   166
15:36-41   25
16:6-10   82
16:14   125
17   31
17:22ff.   70
17:28   107
18:2ff.   125
18:9-10   78, 86
18:24-28   127
18:26   132
21:9   129
27:43   139
28:1-10   139

Romans
1:18-32   11, 48
1:18   15
2:4   42
2:6   20
2:14-15   14, 44,
             48, 63, 138
3:9ff.   109
7:15   12
10:14   80, 89
12:1-9   39f.
12:2   122
12:5   12
12:6-8   145, 147,
             149
12:17-21   144
12:17   40
12:19   40, 60
13:1-4   34-36, 37
13:1-7   40, 59f.,
             69, 74, 135
13:6   43, 46
13:8-10   15, 40f.
14:5-8   30
15:20-21   81
16:1   132
16:2   129

1 Corinthians
6   47
7   130
7:29-31   30
9:19-23   46, 166
11:3,8-9   125
11:5   128
13:12   30
13:13   20
14:33-36   129
14:34   33
15   115
16:2   146
16:9   83
16:13   122

2 Corinthians
4:18   142
5:16   158
5:17   11
8—9   146
8:9   140
8:13-14   99, 101
9:6-8   141
9:7   147

10:4	70
10:16	81

Galatians
2:11-16	166
3:23-24	45
3:28	87, 124
5:6	142
6:10	42, 135, 144, 147, 149

Ephesians
2:8	115
2:10	140
2:14	158
3:10	17
3:20	165
4—6	40
4:12	147
4:14f.	122
4:17-24	166
4:28	99, 100
5:21	122
5:22—6:9	69
6:1-4	109
6:4	61, 110
6:12	17

Philippians
4:8	109

Colossians
1:15	107, 115
1:17	107
2:16	30
3:22-23	98
4:1	98
4:3	83

1 Thessalonians
3:12	135, 147
4:9	99
5:15	135, 147

1 Timothy
1:8-11	45, 46
1:10	162
2:1,2	42, 43, 46, 51, 61f., 69
2:9-15	33
2:9-10	32
2:12	25, 123, 124, 126
2:13	126
2:14	122, 123, 126
2:15	131
3:8-13	149
3:11	129
4:1	49
4:1-10	51
4:8	48
5:3-10	149
5:4	135, 147
5:8	42, 49, 51, 135, 147
5:10	124, 131
5:23	51
6:10	50
6:17-19	50, 51, 141, 147

2 Timothy
1:7	122
2:14-15	123

Titus
2:4	124
2:5	131
2:14	140
3:8	42, 50
3:14	50

Hebrews
12:7-11	109
13:14	30

James
1:27	140
2:14ff.	142, 149
2:18	14, 142
3:9	109
3:17-18	131

1 Peter
1:4	115
1:16	25
2:13-14	35f., 46, 109, 135
2:13—3:7	25
3:1	29, 122
3:7	122
3:14-16	122
4:10-11	14, 145

1 John
2:15-17	49, 166
3:16-20	99, 142, 149
3:18	102
5:2	15

3 John
2	48

Revelation
3:8	161

General Index

Abortion 15, 16, 59, 63, 73, 121
Africa 28, 154
  South Africa 59, 72, 73
Alcohol 47, 73
Anderson, N. 163, 165n.
Association of Christian
  Teachers 118
Atkins, A. 132

Baldwin, J. 18, 20n., 33, 37n.
Barclay, O. R. 21, 53n., 54
Barrett, D. 152, 156, 159f.,
  165n.
Bavinck, J. H. 166
Benington, J. 20n.
Blasphemy 65
Bockmuehl, K. 166
Braund, E. 89
Brown, S. 150
Brueggemann, W. 102n.
Brunner, E. 54
Buddhism 152, 156, 166
Bunyan, John 81

Calvin, John 34, 35, 53n., 75
Capital punishment 13, 25, 59
Capitalism 13, 43, 96
Carey, William 88, 151f., 154f.,
  165
Catherwood, F. 75
Chalmers, Thomas 79f., 89n.,
  150
Christian Socialism 136
Church 39-55
  local 7f., 17-20, 50-2
  church government 17f., 36
  para-church organizations 18

and education 113f., 116f.
Church Action with the
  Unemployed 51, 101, 103n.
Clements, R. 27, 36n., 38
Community work 147f.
Conscience 13, 15f., 31, 44, 60,
  63, 70
Conservatism 7, 12
Coppes, L. J. 150
Creation 31, 42, 47, 50, 97, 107,
  137-9
Culture 23, 25, 28-33, 111, 120,
  124, 126, 160f., 163f.

Dallimore, A. 150
Davies, G. W. 102n.
Deacons 99, 129, 146, 149
Divorce 15, 16, 64, 73, 139

Education 7, 19, 52, 85, 105-18
  of missionary children 15,
    16
  sex education 65
  evolution 65f.
  aims of 106-9
  and parents 111-13
  Christian schools 116f.
  and the church 113f.
Edwards, Jonathan 136, 149n.,
  155, 165
Elderly 15, 16, 42, 51f.
Evangelism 19, 39, 49, 52, 78-81,
  140-3, 151-66
Evans, M. J. 132n.

Fall, the 11f., 19, 27, 42-8, 97f.,
  109f., 124, 126, 139

175

Family, the 98f.
  parenting 42, 52
  and education 105, 110, 111-13
Field, David 14, 20n., 132n.
Foot-washing 31f.
Football violence 13f.
Freeman, D. 102n.

Galbraith, J. K. 75
Gambling 47
Geisler, N. 21
Genocide 26, 27
Gifts 18, 39f., 145f.
Green, W. 103
Greenway, R. 89
Griffiths, B. 102n. 104

Handy, C. 102n., 104
Hendriksen, W. 133
Henry, C. F. H. 102n.
Hill, B. V. 118
Hinduism 152, 154-7, 163, 166
Hirst, P. H. 108, 117n.
Hodge, C. 133
Horn, R. M. 149n.
Hughes, F. 117n., 118
Hurley, J. 37n., 38, 132

Idols 32, 65
Image of God 13f., 25, 31, 70, 97, 109, 137, 139
Inner city 77-89
Islam 152, 155, 156f., 159, 163, 166

Jenkins, D. 93
Johnstone, P. 152
Joslin, R. 89
Jubilee, year of 43, 45, 95
Justice 14f., 16 41, 43, 45f., 71f.

Kaye, B. N. 21, 35, 36n., 37, 38
Kenosis 66f.
Kidner, D. 14, 20n.
Kingdom of God 42f., 44
Kraemer, H. 156, 165n.
Kuyper, A. 54

Langley, M. 132
Law 26-8, 40, 45f., 62
  legalism 19, 26f.,
Lees, S. 132
Lenski, R. C. H. 126, 128, 131, 133
Lesser evil 15f., 46-8, 139
Lloyd-Jones, D. M. 20n., 37f., 89n., 133
Local church — see Church
London City Mission 89
London Institute For Contemporary Christianity 55
Love 40f., 67
Lyon, D. 17, 20n.

MacLeod, D. M. 149n.
MacMurray, J. 74n., 75
Manton, M. 132n.
Marriage 29, 30f., 45
  remarriage 15, 16
  polygamy 32
Marshall, H. 25, 26, 29, 36n., 37
Martin, C. 118
Marty, M. E. 149n.
Marxism 17, 59, 66, 106, 157-60, 166
May, P. 118
Mental handicap 52, 147
Meyer, F. B. 84
Mission 151-66
  call to 15
  and women 128
  and prayer 164f.
Morgan, C. 79
Motyer, J. A. 14, 20n., 21, 149n.
Murray, I. 164
Murray, J. 23, 36n.
Music 31
Mysticism 19

Neighbours 11-13, 14f., 39, 53, 63
Newbigin, L. 166
Nida, E. 166
Niebuhr, R. 66f., 72, 74n., 75

Northern Ireland 59, 73, 92
Nostalgia 19f.

Oates, Captain 15, 16
Olyott, S. 13, 150

Packer, J. 13, 20n., 21, 25, 32,
  36n., 37
Peace 45f., 48, 61
Pearson, G. 20n.
Peters, R. S. 106, 107, 117n.
Peterson, M. L. 118
Pluralism 62f., 65, 157
Politics 13, 27, 34f., 43, 47f., 59
  (see also State)
  and the church 50, 67-74
  Christ's teaching 68
  Christian objectives in 46-8,
    61-3, 70f.
  and unemployment 101f.
Pornography 40, 52
Potter, D. 150
Poverty 7, 72, 142, 145
  'deserving poor' 140
Prayer 19, 61, 69, 83f., 112,
  164f.
Preaching 32, 49, 69, 73, 80f.
Prior, D. 133
Property 63f.
Prostitution 47, 80, 85

Race 13, 86-8, 158
Redemption 12, 115f., 139f.
Revival 18-20, 46
Richards, J. R. 132
Righteousness 14f., 16, 41, 45f.,
  47
Rights 14
Rushdoony, R. J. 36n.
Rutherford, Samuel 75

Schaeffer, F. 75, 102n.
Schluter, M. 27, 36n., 38
Scripture
  authority of 13, 17, 23-38, 73
  regulative principle 18, 36
  Old Testament 23, 26-8, 43,
    44

principles of 13, 24-6, 30, 32,
  123
interpretation of 25f., 34-6,
  124-6
Secularization 93-6
Shaftesbury Project 54
Shaw, I. 150
Simeon, Charles 53
Simon, P. 31
Single parents 7
Slavery 33, 36, 44f., 48, 97
Smith, D. 30, 37n.
Smith, R. 104
Social gospel 136
Social welfare
  and the local church 143-8
  and evangelism 140-3, 144f.,
    149, 162f.
  and the state 145f.
Social work 39, 47, 50
Solzhenitsyn, A. 71f., 74n., 159
Spurgeon, C. 150
State 15, 16, 17, 26, 34-36, 40f.,
  59-75 (see also Politics)
  government 33, 42, 44f.
Stonehouse, N. 37
Storkey, A. 54
Storkey, E. 132
Stott, J. 11, 17, 20n., 21, 30,
  54, 55, 125, 132n., 133
Structural sin 17, 44 (see also
  Fall)
Studd, C. T. 84, 151
Sunday 40, 46, 64f., 94-6
Sunday, Billy 136
Sutcliff, John 165

Taylor, Hudson 151
Taylor, R. 166
Taxation 26, 60
Terminal illness 148
Third world 62, 153-7
Thomas, John 154f.
Thompson, P. 89
Tradition 120
Triton, A. N. 21, 54
Truth 16, 63

Unemployment — see Work

Voting 68

Wallis, J. 20n.
Walls, A. F. 102n.
Walter, J. A. 75, 166
Ward, William 155
Washington, George 66
Wenham, G. J. 21, 36n., 37
Westminster Confession 23, 24, 66
Williams, William 155
Wilmer, H. 34, 35, 37n., 75
Winwood, D. J. 104
Wilson, B. 160, 161, 165n.
Women
  in the local church 119-33
  oppression of 121
  male/female qualities 122f.
  Women's Liberation 119, 121,
    132
  and preaching 123-6
  ministry of 126-9
  single women 130
  and employment of married
    women 130
Work
  Christian doctrine of 97-102
  in a secular society 93-6
  unemployment 7, 18, 51f., 59,
    71, 73, 91-3, 100f., 144
Worldliness 48-50
Wright, C. 28, 36n., 38
Wright, D. F. 75

de Yong, P. Y. 150

Zink, D. 30, 37n.

NOTES

NOTES

A companion volume to *Social Issues and the Local Church*
published by the Evangelical Press of Wales

CHRISTIAN FAMILY MATTERS
Family Life — A Biblical Viewpoint

Edited by
Ian Shaw

The Christian today is nowhere faced with a more acute challenge
to think and live to the honour of God than in the sphere of the
family. During the post-war period a significant shift of attitude
towards the family has taken place. The dramatic growth in the rate
of divorce and abortion is perhaps the most prominent indicator of
the increasing fragmentation of the family unit in society today. In
the face of this social quicksand, Christians are called to defend
and exemplify not 'traditional' values, but the biblical view of the
family. It is our responsibility to apply God's unchanging Word to
a changing society.

To this end it is essential that we understand clearly what God's
Word says about marriage and the family, and that we rest on
Scripture alone. Without this foundation we shall be at sea in face
of the current onslaught on traditional views and values. This book
endeavours to provide such a foundation. Each contributor seeks
to draw out the biblical principles relevant to his particular area,
and their application today. As Sir Fred Catherwood indicates in
his Foreword, their aim is to shine a light in the increasing darkness
of the unhappy society in which we live.

CONTENTS

- **The Bible and the Family** Ian Shaw
- **The Marriage Covenant** J. Elwyn Davies
- **Parenthood** Douglas D. Jones
- **Childhood and Adolescence** David P. Kingdon
- **The Handicapped Child** David C. Potter
- **Fostering and Adoption** Stuart Olyott
- **The Elderly and the Church** Ian Shaw
- **Divorce** Neil C. Richards
- **Abortion and Family Planning** Brian Harris

The Christian, the Church and Daily Work

Gerallt Wyn Davies

In this little book the author looks at biblical teaching regarding work, compares it with society's attitudes, and outlines what individual Christians and the church could do to be of effective help in alleviating the great social problem of unemployment.

The Christian Heritage of Welsh Education

R. M. Jones & Gwyn Davies

A bird's-eye view of Christian education in Wales through the centuries, together with a wealth of fascinating extracts from contemporary books and magazines relating to Christianity and education in Wales in the period 1700-1900.